make great decisions Christian workbook for teen girls

make great decisions Christian workbook for teen girls

A PRACTICAL & BIBLICAL GUIDE TO CHOICES THAT MATTER

Jocasta Odom

ROCKRIDGE PRESS

I would like to dedicate this book to my boys, Connor and Dylan. Their strong walk with God has encouraged me to write for the young teens of their generation. Also, to my students for showing me what is missing in their world.

For general information on our other products and services or to obtain technical support, please contact our Customer Care Department within the United States at (866) 744-2665, or outside the United States at (510) 253-0500.

Rockridge Press publishes its books in a variety of electronic and print formats. Some content that appears in print may not be available in electronic books, and vice versa.

Interior and Cover Designer: Suzanne LaGasa
Art Producer: Janice Ackerman
Editor: Adrienne Ingrum
Production Editor: Jenna Dutton

Arlene Brathwaite / Queens Eye Photography, p.130

ISBN: Print 978-1-64611-127-5 | eBook 978-1-64611-128-2

CONTENTS

A Helpful Hint about Bible Quotations

You don't need a Bible to enjoy this book. The discussions include quotations from the Bible, but it will help if you have a Bible, a Bible app, or access to the Internet. Many Bible apps are free. Search "Bible" in an app store on your phone, tablet, laptop, or computer; you'll discover more choices than you can imagine. Many church websites also include Bibles.

The Bible is a compilation of **66 books**. When you check out the contents page of a Bible, you'll see the names of those books start with Genesis and end with Revelation.

Each book of the Bible is divided into **chapters**.

Each chapter is divided into **verses**.

Scripture references are made by book, chapter, and verse. For example, Genesis 2:4 means the book of Genesis, chapter 2, verse 4.

Sometimes, letters appear after a Scripture reference. For example, Genesis 2:4 (NIV). Those letters refer to the **translation** of the Bible—the New International Version, in this case.

The Bible is an ancient book. It was not originally written in English, but it's been translated for those of us who read English. Many, many translators have put those ancient words into our language. And, just like you might say "Hello," "Hi," "Howdy," "Yo," "Hey," "Whassup," or some other greeting, different translators have chosen different words to convey the meaning of those ancient languages. This book uses several Bible translations in hopes that you will easily understand what God is saying in each Scripture quoted. You'll find the list of translations used in the back of this book (see Biblical Citations on page 129).

Chapter 1

Oh My Gosh! Another Decision!

Choose for yourselves this day whom you will serve. . . . But as for me and my household, we will serve the Lord. (Joshua 24:15, NIV)

God loves you so much. The Almighty created you and sent Jesus so that you can live eternally. Still, with all the power in the universe, God doesn't force decisions on you. The Creator has given you great potential and a powerful mind. You can choose for yourself whether to love God and others, positively impact your world, live the wonderful life that is possible for you, and do it all by trusting God's wisdom to help you make great decisions. You've got this!

EACH DAY, FROM THE MOMENT YOU WAKE . . .

With the chime of your cell phone alarm, a series of decisions begins about everything, from whether you'll check Snapchat before rolling out of bed to what you'll wear to school or how long you'll study for next week's biology exam. As hours pass, you'll make some good and some bad decisions—like M&M's and Doritos for lunch (guilty!)—but, mostly, you're not hurting anything, right? The longer-term stuff, like where you live and your finances, is not fully up to you yet; you're still a teenager—*geez*! Even if you don't feel totally in control, or you think you have time to figure things out, you're on the verge of the big (sometimes scary) transition into adulthood. It's time to get ready!

> This is the day the Lord has made. We will rejoice and be glad in it. (Psalm 118:24, NLT)

You've probably heard this verse. Simply put: God has made each day. In truth, there is something in each day to be happy about. No matter what situations or choices you face in a day—good, bad, or scary—the One who made it will see you through. Making great choices as you begin each day will position you to live with strength and positivity.

Your Best Start

How can you start your day right, ready to handle any challenge it brings? Think about your routine and the first things you generally do each day (aside from restroom necessities, obviously). Do you wake up early, scroll Instagram, eat a healthy breakfast, take time to greet your family, or pray? Write it down (see My Current Routine)! Then, consider whether these activities are best for preparing your mind, body, and spirit for the day ahead. What other things might you try instead? Write it down (see My New Morning Routine), make adjustments to your current routine, and follow it for a few days to see what happens. Even simple, positive choices can have a big payoff. Give each day your best start!

My Current Routine	**My New Morning Routine**
_____	_____
_____	_____
_____	_____
_____	_____
_____	_____

Continue to reassess your choices about how you spend your mornings as you grow through reading this book. Bonus tip: Write Psalm 118:24 on a note card or sticky paper and put it on your mirror. For some a.m. positivity, read it aloud each morning when you first look in the mirror as you're getting ready for the day.

Write a Prayer

According to Psalm 17:6, your needs will be heard: "I call on you, my God, for you will answer me; turn your ear to me and hear my prayer" (NIV). While you're contemplating your routine, here's a not-so-subtle suggestion for incorporating prayer. Even if you already pray every morning, think about the current concerns and situations you're facing now. God hears you and cares. Invite God's presence into your daily decision-making. In the space provided, write a brief prayer that you can memorize and repeat as needed in the morning or throughout the day. It doesn't have to be fancy; just write from your heart as though you're addressing a friend, because that's what Jesus is (John 15:13)!

Dear Lord,

_____

_____

_____

_____

Think about It

Keep your minds on whatever is true, pure, right, holy, friendly, and proper. Don't ever stop thinking about what is truly worthwhile and worthy of praise. . . . And God, who gives peace, will be with you. (Philippians 4:8–9, CEV)

When you focus on what is good, the Lord is with you. Good thoughts, good decisions, and good outcomes fit together. Sure, you make decisions constantly, but how often do you really consider how your choices today will affect your future? Ever jump in on a little online hating? Skip class now and again? No biggie—except it is. You can't go back to being a kid—that time when decisions were few and easy! Yet you've not quite launched into a real-world adulthood, either. You're somewhere in between, where it can be tough. It's hard to grasp how much *your* decisions matter when caregivers speak into your life and choices. Perhaps you're waiting for your chance to be an adult—for your life to start—before you think too much about your choices. Right now, and as you get older, your choices are projecting your identity. The decisions you make now can impact everything from your sense of happiness to the kinds of opportunities you'll have. Think about it: Someone who regularly makes it to class on time and works at their grades is going to be considered by teachers for internship recommendations before someone who doesn't. Decisions about how you treat others not only affect you but also have the power to impact others in a lasting way (being the butt of the joke is a real self-esteem crusher). Trust me, you don't want to be caught off guard as things get more *real* (and it's no longer your homework but your rent that's late). Even at your age, *you* and *your actions* matter. You are full of potential to shine.

You will harvest what you plant. (Galatians 6:7, CEV)

Your decisions are like seeds—smart, conscientious choices grow good fruit like strong faith, kindness, peace, a solid reputation, a stable future, and loving relationships. It's easy to underestimate the power of little choices and behaviors. Acting on impulse is easy to do, especially when you're joining in what others are doing. But the better the seeds you plant now, the better your future rewards will be.

Assess Your Decision-Making

This exercise will help you assess how intentional you're being in decision-making. Godly choices about how you fuel your body and mind (both holy aspects of your being), how you spend your time, and how you treat others will help you reach your best potential. Put a check beside each statement that applies to you. Be honest!

Group A

☐ I read books that are inspiring and challenge me to think.

☐ I choose movies and television shows that aren't too explicit or filled with vulgar language.

☐ I listen to music that makes me happy and feel good about myself.

☐ I try to disperse a group of gossipers who run down someone who's not around.

☐ I am proud to admit my own interests.

☐ I'm honest with my parents and respect their rules.

☐ I make an effort to be punctual to class and solid in attendance.

☐ I eat fruits and vegetables as much as possible (or palatable).

☐ I make daily prayer a priority.

☐ I make an effort to get to church.

☐ If someone is being picked on, I speak up.

☐ I'm waiting to share the most intimate things with my future spouse.

☐ I study hard.

Group B

☐ I read fashion mags (bonus: sex tips).

☐ I watch popular cable TV shows, even if they freak me out a little, so I can talk about them with friends.

☐ I listen to songs with great beats even though the lyrics sometimes make me uncomfortable.

☐ I sometimes join in when friends are gossiping, but I don't mean any harm.

☐ I sometimes pretend to like things I don't to fit in.

☐ On occasion, I lie to my parents about where I'll be.

☐ I am often late to class.

☐ I eat a lot of junk food and drink a lot of soda. Green smoothie? Hard pass!

☐ I pray now and then.

☐ I go to church when I have to.

- ☐ If someone is being picked on, I try not to get involved. I don't want to become the target!

- ☐ I text guys sexy messages or photos of myself.

- ☐ I study enough to get by.

See a lot of Group B checks? Don't worry (you're pretty relatable). Even by taking time to self-assess, you are already getting wiser. You can revisit this exercise after you've finished this book to see your progress. The goal is to eventually see more checks by Group A statements.

Assess the Impact of Your Decisions

Review the example decisions from the previous exercise, and write down a potential outcome or effect from that choice in the spaces provided.

I read books that are inspiring and challenge me to think.

_____

I choose movies and television shows that aren't too explicit or filled with vulgar language.

_____

I listen to music that makes me happy and feel good about myself.

_____

I try to disperse a group of gossipers who run someone down when they're not around.

_____

I am proud to admit my own interests.

_____

I'm honest with my parents and respect their rules.

_____

I make an effort to be punctual to class and solid in attendance.

_____

I eat fruits and vegetables as much as possible (or palatable).

_____

I make daily prayer a priority.

_____

I make an effort to get to church.

_____

If someone is being picked on, I speak up.

_____

I'm waiting to share the most intimate things with my future spouse.

_____

I study hard.

_____

I read fashion mags (bonus: sex tips).

_____

I watch popular cable TV shows, even if they freak me out a little, so I can talk about them with friends.

_____

I listen to songs with great beats even though the lyrics sometimes make me uncomfortable.

_____

I sometimes join in when friends are gossiping, but I don't mean any harm.

_____

I sometimes pretend to like things I don't to fit in.

_____

On occasion, I lie to my parents about where I'll be.

_____

I am often late to class.

_____

I eat a lot of junk food and drink a lot of soda. Green smoothie? Hard pass!

_____

I pray now and then.

_____

I go to church when I have to.

_____

If someone is being picked on, I try not to get involved. I don't want to become the target!

_____

I text guys sexy messages or photos of myself.

_____

I study enough to get by.

_____

Now, consider how your choices could affect your spiritual, mental, social, and physical well-being. This is practice for thinking about the power of your choices.

We know how much God loves us, and we have put our trust in his love. God is love, and all who live in love live in God, and God lives in them.
(1 John 4:16, NLT)

It's reassuring to know how much God cares. You can put your trust in God's never-ending, unconditional love. If you ever feel that something has gone so wrong you can't come back from it or you can't talk to anyone about it, you can trust that God will always understand and be happy to hear from you. Also, think of someone in your life who you know really loves God and confide in that person. Every adult was once a teen. You might be surprised how much they can relate to you—no matter what you're facing!

MISTAKES ARE NORMAL

Just like everyone else, you're going to feel great about some choices, and others might feel like mistakes. God still loves you no matter what you do. That love can't be undone. God is eternal and unchanging (Hebrews 13:8), and so is God's love for you!

Always let him lead you, and he will clear the road for you to follow. (Proverbs 3:6, CEV)

Decisions aren't always easy, but it's best to do what's right, even when it's hard. Do it with the help of your Creator, who promises to make the right choices clearer because every decision matters.

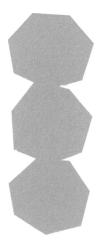

EVERY DECISION MATTERS

Big and little, *every* choice has an implication. A seemingly insignificant, though not-so-great, choice can become a bad habit. Good habits lead to good days that become a peaceful life. Sometimes, even *not* deciding can have an impact, like choosing to stay quiet when you witness an injustice. It's smart to practice making good choices right now, in everything you do. Why? That's how you take control of your future and who you want to be. Your choices reflect your identity. Own it! Believe in yourself and your power to make great decisions, but don't be discouraged by a snag here or there. You will make mistakes, and a bad choice does not define who you are. You're aiming for an awareness that choices matter. Try your best to make good ones and get back on track when you (inevitably) struggle at times.

> I will bless you with a future filled with
> hope—a future of success, not of suffering.
> (Jeremiah 29:11, CEV)

As a child of the generous, loving Creator, your future definitely looks bright. Can you picture it?

My Choices, My Future

Take a moment to visualize who you want to be, spiritually, in ten years—as a friend, professionally, anything! What good choices will help you get there? List your answers in the columns below after the example.

Desired Characteristic

Good Choices

I have a close relationship with Jesus.

I choose daily prayer over other activities.

_____   _____

_____   _____

_____   _____

_____   _____

> But anyone who needs wisdom should ask God, whose very nature is to give to everyone without a second thought, without keeping score. Wisdom will certainly be given to those who ask. (James 1:5, CEB)

How do you make a good decision, especially when it's tricky? As humans, we're learning all the time, but there is a limit to our knowledge. Not so with God. The wisdom of the Almighty is infinite, and your generous Creator doesn't want you to suffer over a decision. Without a doubt, you will be given the wisdom you need to navigate your choices if you ask for it and invite God more deeply into the process. This kind of wisdom will even help you recover and grow from past decisions you wish you could take back.

In the space provided, write a brief prayer that you can memorize and repeat as needed when you face a tough decision. Be real. When you're tempted, this prayer will come in handy. It doesn't have to be fancy; write from your heart as though you're addressing a friend, because that's what Jesus is (John 15:13)!

Dear Lord,

_____

_____

_____

_____

_____

LEARNING FROM DECISIONS

When you make a decision you regret, it's okay! You have a choice in how to respond. And what you learn from not-so-great choices has big value for your future. Mistakes might even give you an opportunity to make a tough, but wonderful, decision, like admitting when you're wrong or apologizing to someone. Responding well to mistakes, even when it's hard, keeps you on the right path for your future and will make you feel so much better—trust me! It's a big sign of growth and maturity.

How to Make a Good Decision: CHECKLIST

Struggling with a big or small decision? Here's a checklist of things you can do to help you make the best choice for you:

☐ Pray about it! Talk to God daily about a specific decision and ask for the wisdom you need.

☐ Give it time! Don't act hastily if you're unsure what decision to make. Wait until you feel great about your decision before you act.

☐ Read the Bible—your roadmap for life and another source of godly wisdom.

☐ Turn to a trusted adult for advice, like a parent, teacher, pastor, or counselor.

☐ Consider the possible short- and long-term effects of the decision.

☐ Make a list of the potential positive and negative results.

☐ Do not be pressured or persuaded! It's your decision. (Repeat after me: "It's *my* decision!")

TO SUM UP

God wants to help you make smart decisions. Because God loves you, your Creator wants you to experience the benefits of a close, strong spiritual relationship. Seek God's wisdom because decisions are tough! Today, teens face a host of problems unique to your generation—the first one that has always lived with the pressures of social media. Remember, God is love (1 John 4:8); the Creator loves you through your good and bad decisions. God will not leave you for any reason. So never beat yourself up—just dust yourself off. You, my dear, are amazing. And I'm here to help you know and grow in God's love for you. In everything—from your roles at home and school to your friendships and romantic relationships and even what your personal style says about you—the Scripture, ideas, and exercises in this workbook will help you become a master decision maker!

Chapter 2

It's My Time to Shine

You are the light of the world. A town built on a hill cannot be hidden. Neither do people light a lamp and put it under a bowl. Instead they put it on its stand, and it gives light to everyone in the house. In the same way, let your light shine before others, that they may see your good deeds and glorify your Father in heaven. (Matthew 5:14–16, NIV)

You are a beloved child of God. But as a believer in a modern world, you likely face challenges that can impact your decision-making. From peer pressure to doing things that don't seem to fit with your beliefs, temptations on the Internet, or academic pressure that comes between you and your devotion to church or friends or family, you face tough choices. Who doesn't want to fit in? Who wants to feel *different*?

Even if some people don't understand, it's important to remember the amazing person you are in Christ—that person is going to make some excellent, if not always popular, choices for a great life. As you ease into adulthood and make decisions that will shape your future, know that it's your time to shine. Be kind to yourself. Enjoy learning and growing while you become the woman God created you to be.

You are not made to be hidden. Your faith and connection to Christ, the most amazing part of your identity, are meant to sparkle from within. Through kind words and actions, you can reflect Christ's love to anyone, wherever you go. Talk about special!

TO UNDERSTAND WHO AND WHOSE YOU ARE IS KEY

You're pretty special. God lives in you (Galatians 2:20). Your belief in God comes with access to supernatural (spiritual) support and strength in everything. All you have to do is invite the Almighty to help. Like everyone has done at some point, if you ever make a decision that doesn't reflect your identity in God, the Lord has ways of reintroducing you to yourself. The Holy Spirit will be at your side through troubled times and good times. You can accept the gift of God's promise to be your refuge, your strength, and a present help in struggle (Psalms 46:1).

Shine Like a Diamond: TRUE OR FALSE QUIZ

What choices do you make that reflect your inner light? This quiz will help you figure out what decisions are helping you shine and if they reflect your identity in Christ. Circle "True" or "False" for each of the following statements.

I try not to use vulgar language, even if it's used by others around me.

    True   **False**

I dress in a way that gives me confidence, but I don't show my body to impress guys.

    True   **False**

If a friend needs my help, I try to support them—even if I've got a lot going on in my life, too.

    True   **False**

Before I post on social media, I ask myself whether this photo reflects my self-respect and how it might impact my reputation or future opportunities.

    True   **False**

Before I comment on social media, I ask myself whether my words are hurtful or kind.

    True   **False**

I make family a priority even though I'm busy or would sometimes rather do other things.

True   **False**

I volunteer or step up when there is a need—holding doors for the elderly, sharing food, or

helping _____ (for example, my little brother) with homework.

True   **False**

Even if we don't always agree, I try to be respectful and understanding of my parents.

True   **False**

I respect my principal, teachers, and classmates, and I try to keep a positive attitude
about my assignments.

True   **False**

I can lose gracefully and celebrate others' victories.

True   **False**

I try not to let comparison and jealousy take over or impact the way I treat others.

True   **False**

I speak up if I see something bad happen to someone else.

True   **False**

I tell others about Jesus's love.

True   **False**

Mark a reminder on your calendar or set one in your phone to take this quiz again in
one month, and again in a month after that, aiming for more "true" answers each time.
Celebrate the fact that you're radiating good vibes wherever you go!

I Won't Hide: PRAYER

God will help you feel more and more comfortable letting your faith be shown to others—through either words or good actions. Write a brief prayer asking for confidence to live out every aspect of who you are. Memorize this prayer and repeat it whenever you're in a situation where you want to shine, but it feels easier to hide or try to blend into the crowd.

Dear Jesus,

_____

_____

_____

_____

> We know that God is always at work for the good of everyone who loves him. They are the ones God has chosen for his purpose. (Romans 8:28, CEV)

Sometimes it might feel like nobody cares or understands. Maybe you're on the outs with a friend, or your mom is coming down hard on you, or your teachers have difficult expectations and want you to figure out how to make the grade. These situations are tough, but God never rests. Your Creator is always working to make something good for your life from what seems impossible right now. The Almighty turns hurdles into growth of your character, faith, and problem-solving skills. Knowing that God is not sitting out any lap of your race will give you the boost you need to make godly choices. Try your best amidst the struggle. Keep jogging, and walk when you have to—God's going to see you through to the finish line!

EVERYONE FEELS INSECURE ABOUT WHO THEY ARE FROM TIME TO TIME

If you've noticed something another girl has—her clothes, her hair, her popularity—and you wish it was yours, chances are there's someone feeling the same way about you! When you feel envy or self-doubt creeping in, remember your own significance and what's special about you. We're all made to shine in our own unique ways. Be reassured by the fact that God is always at work for *you*, always looking out for your future. And no matter the great or not-so-great decisions you make along the way, God will use each of them for your good to help you grow. You have an incredible, chosen purpose; nothing changes that.

> Test yourselves *to see* if you are in the faith; examine yourselves!... (2 Corinthians 13:5, NASB)

The Bible encourages self-reflection to gauge if our lives and decisions reflect our faith and if we're being our best. Let the next exercise help you evaluate your faith and build a deeper appreciation for yourself.

To Know Me Is to Love Me

The key to loving who you are is knowing what makes you unique. Let's bring that self-awareness to the surface and highlight your interests, skills, and positive personality traits. Fill in the blanks with your answers.

My favorite subject in school is _____.

My least favorite subject in school is _____.

I _____ *better than anyone in my family.*

When someone needs _____, *they come to me.*

My friends say that they most like _____ *about me.*

_____ *is an activity that makes me happy; while doing this, hours could pass without my knowing it.*

I most like _____ *about my best girlfriend.*

I most like _____ *about my best guy friend.*

The career of my dreams is _____.

_____ *is an activity that makes me feel good about myself.*

My dream vacation is going to _____,

and when I get there I plan to _____ _____.

An experience when I've felt God's presence most strongly is _____.

The thing about myself I want to work on most is _____.

Hopefully, this exercise has given you a focused glimpse of yourself—how guided you are by faith, your likes, what activities make you happiest and fuel your spirit, what you value in those closest to you, and your goals. Repeat this quiz in a notebook as often as you'd like, adding more than one answer if you want to. By examining yourself and staying connected with who you are, it'll be natural to make choices that are true to you.

If you plan and work hard, you will have plenty . . .
(Proverbs 21:5, CEV)

Turn to any page in the Bible, and you'll find timeless wisdom and commonsense reminders for life. Sure, getting wealthy from your YouTube channel featuring you testing makeup in your pajamas sounds like a great gig, but there really is no surer way to have what you need in life than by planning and hard work.

GOOD PLANNING AND HARD WORK ARE A SURE COMBINATION FOR HAPPINESS AND SUCCESS

Short-term goals, like good grades on your finals, are opportunities to test the power of planning and smart choices. True, reaching your goals will sometimes require sacrifices, like occasionally skipping a fun party to study. For longer-term goals, the sacrifices might be greater, like working over the summer to save up to buy a car. The beauty of developing your goal-setting, planning, and choice-making now is that you'll undoubtedly carry these skills into the future. It also shows you how much you can accomplish when you set your mind to something and work for it. You are capable. You will have plenty. You will be super proud.

> But Jesus looked at them and said, "With man this is impossible, but with God all things are possible."
> (Matthew 19:26, ESV)

Don't be afraid to follow your heart—to set and work at your goals (even for that YouTube channel!)—no matter how grand your ambition may be. There is purpose in the pursuit. You're carving your own unique path. Your goals may change as you grow, and where you end up could be even better than your best dream. The point is to set goals, reach for them, and keep dreaming. You'll get where you're meant to be. With God beside you, it's all possible.

Life Lessons: SETTING SHORT-TERM AND LONG-TERM GOALS

This exercise will help you set some personal short-term and long-term goals. By setting goals and making choices to help you achieve them, you're preparing yourself for present and future success.

Short-Term Goals   **Long-Term Goals**

_____   _____

_____   _____

_____   _____

_____   _____

_____   _____

Revisit your short-term goals every 30 days until all have been completed. Also, track the steps you're taking toward your long-term goals by keeping them updated in a journal.

> Consider it pure joy, my brothers and sisters, whenever you face trials of many kinds, because you know that the testing of your faith produces perseverance. (James 1:2–3, NIV)

It's hard to get happy about facing challenges in your faith, with your friends and family, or at school—am I right? It is not, however, impossible. Confronting tough things that challenge your faith can produce in you a key ingredient for a successful life: perseverance. Not to minimize your personal trials—only you know how difficult they are—but leaning on the Lord's strength will make you stronger than your struggles. Things might be tough, but you and God together are tougher. You're growing as a person, and you should be proud of yourself.

PURSUING GOALS COMES WITH CHALLENGES

Inevitably, you'll face setbacks or rejection, and you'll take some wrong turns. No struggle is wasted! You're building perseverance and learning to pick yourself up from the effects of mistakes, bad luck, or the attacks of others. Regardless of your circumstances or the people who get in the way of what you want, aim for inner peace and practice not letting your emotions cloud your decision-making. You've hit a bump in the road; it doesn't have to send you into a ditch. Stay in your lane, do the best you can, and persevere! God won't give up on you (Joshua 1:5), so don't give up on yourself.

> For God gave us a spirit not of fear but of power and love and self-control. (2 Timothy 1:7, ESV)

You are made with a spirit to endure and face difficult decisions bravely and to do so without losing control.

I Will Not Lose Control of Myself

Decision-making can be especially tough when emotions are involved. Maybe you're having trouble in a friendship, being asked to keep a dangerous secret, or torn between paths. You're going to do the right thing, but that doesn't mean it's not emotionally exhausting. Here's an idea that might help: Do an online search for the Serenity Prayer, commonly attributed to Reinhold Niebuhr. You will likely find the prayer in its entirety, as well as a shorter version that's about four lines long. Write the shorter version on the lines provided.

_____

_____

_____

_____

Recite the prayer whenever you need help remaining calm as you persevere. Sometimes, a good reminder that the Lord is actually in control, and not us, is what we need to alleviate pressure and keep ourselves together. God's got you, and you're in good hands!

GOD'S CREATIVITY IS IN ME

In his hand is the life of every creature and the breath of all mankind. (Job 12:10, NIV)

The creativity of the Creator of the universe is so amazing—by God, all things exist, and in an endlessly beautiful and diverse way. That creativity is part of you, too. Your creativity affects how you see the world, how you think, what you make of your circumstances, and how you choose to go about almost everything. It's a great tool for helping you navigate life.

Does My Favorite Color Best Describe My Personality?

This fun exercise will help you tap into the power of your creativity by considering what color you're drawn to. Circle your favorite of the following colors:

ORANGE **BLACK** BLUE **RED** **GREY** WHITE **PURPLE** GREEN

Now, go to https://visme.co/blog/colors-effects-on-mood-emotions/ to see the color-personality chart and article by Suzanne Vallance.

Are you and your color a pair? If not, it doesn't mean you need to choose a different favorite color—only that you should pay more attention to your color and how you feel when you wear it or even use it to decorate. Any color you gravitate toward and choose to fill your life with should add to your joy.

GOD IN MIND

Don't be like the people of this world, but let God
change the way you think. Then you will know how
to do everything that is good and pleasing to him.
(Romans 12:2, CEV)

The condition of your mind is important to your life, and it's key to figuring out what's
best for you. The Bible encourages us to keep our minds on what's good in God's sight—
not what the world around us says is good—and to let our minds be made new. To really
care for your thought center means taking time to be alone with God and your thoughts.
That's known as quiet time or "Me Time."

Me Time

Self-care is helpful to clear thinking and good decision-making. The most transforming
self-care you can give yourself is time alone with God's Holy Spirit. Teens are subjected to
information overload on a daily basis—at home and at school and through large and small
screens. The information is not always joyful and often scary; this can be overwhelming
and make it harder to process life and maintain good thoughts. This step-by-step exercise
will encourage renewing meditation.

Step 1: Turn off your phone. The phone being on will only distract you from launching
fully into your Me Time.

Step 2: Grab the Bible (one made with paper; Bible apps are great, but for this exercise,
go old-school if you can). This will allow you to have my best resource available if
a concern comes to mind and you need biblical answers.

Step 3: Go to a quiet place. This can be your room, the library, or even the bathroom or
a closet if you need to.

Step 4: Play some soft instrumental music. This step is optional, but it's encouraged to
help you relax. If your music is on your phone, turn off the ringer, alerts, and
pop-ups.

Step 5: Sit quietly and take a deep breath from your nose, counting slowly as you release the air through your mouth. Do this for five to ten minutes your first time, and increase your Me Time by five minutes each session thereafter until you find your best fit.

Step 6: As thoughts come to your mind, let them flow through, but do not linger on them. Consider them like birds landing on a branch—your mind—and then flying off. Don't let them nest. Use your Bible to find verses for concerns you can't let flow out of your mind and find biblical answers.

This is a great, renewing exercise. Even though it's focused "Me Time," God is there with you. Don't worry about a formal prayer to acknowledge God, unless you want to. Rather, just know your Lord is there and can sense your heart. In the silence, think of specific concerns you'd like to share with God. Commit to this exercise as a brief routine for the rest of your life. Me Time will allow you to exit your daily frustrations and release the stresses they cause. It will help you renew your mind so that God's will is clear, and that will boost your decision-making.

WOW GOD!

I praise you because I am fearfully and wonderfully made; your works are wonderful, I know that full well. (Psalm 139:14, NIV)

You are a wonderful creation of God. Let your choices in how you celebrate who you are honor your Creator.

I Will Speak Positivity over My Life

You are more than worthy; you are fearfully and wonderfully made. Take fifteen seconds to speak some of these positive, affirming Scriptures aloud:

I am more than a conqueror. (Romans 8:37)

I can do all things through Christ who strengthens me. (Philippians 4:13)

I will not lose heart. (Romans 5:4–5)

I walk in God's truth. (Psalm 26:2–4)

God will never test me beyond my endurance. (1 Corinthians 10:12–14)

Jesus has done so much for me, so I will always give him thanks. (Psalm 100:4–5)

No one else's opinions matter because Jesus is my comforter. (Isaiah 51:12)

I will learn to listen to the Lord, for God knows me better than I know myself. (Romans 8:26)

Surely goodness and mercy shall follow me all the days of my life. (Psalms 23:6)

I encourage you to do this exercise every day, even when you're not in the mood. Or record your voice on your phone's recorder app and play it back to yourself on days you're not in the mood. You'll be amazed at the power you have to impact your own outlook by speaking positively to yourself.

PUTTING ME NOT FIRST

Instead of being motivated by selfish ambition or vanity, each of you should, in humility, be moved to treat one another as more important than yourself. Each of you should be concerned not only about your own interests, but about the interests of others as well. (Philippians 2:3–4, NET)

The Bible clearly instructs us away from selfish choices and toward generosity and concern for others.

YOU WIN WHEN YOU'RE SELFLESS

Perhaps, especially at this time in your life, it's hard to choose to serve the needs of others over your own. You might even be hearing that this is "your time to be selfish" before you have responsibility to care for your own family. But selfishness was never part of God's design for how to live a full and successful life. Even though the world advertises the material benefits of living for yourself or living to *get yours*, doing so will keep you from experiencing the richness of all God can accomplish through you. You were made for community and to play a role in the Kingdom of God. Giving attention to the needs of others won't jeopardize your own success. If you're too focused on yourself and not focused enough on those around you, you'll miss out on the exciting story you could be writing together with your lives. If you live for God, others, and yourself, the opportunities God presents to you will never disappoint.

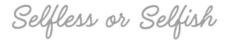

This exercise will help you gauge whether you act more selflessly or selfishly. Consider the statements provided and circle those that apply to you.

I never like doing little things for others.	I love to help out when I see others need it.
I put what I have to do first.	My priorities can wait, when necessary.
I don't know what God expects from me.	I work at doing what I think pleases God.
I am too busy to volunteer at church.	I volunteer at church whenever I can.
I don't have time to listen to what others have to say.	I try my best to be a listening ear to others.
I feel uncomfortable talking about Jesus to others.	I love when I get the opportunity to talk about Jesus.

If you have circled more boxes on the right, you are all about being selfless. If not, don't worry. Just jump in the next time an opportunity presents itself to experience the joy of a selfless choice. That might mean doing something for someone else, and you could be surprised to discover what a blessing it is for yourself.

TO SUM UP

Teen years are exciting, but they can also be confusing and overwhelming. As you navigate mixed signals and scary choices while trying to find your way, it's important to take some time to yourself and center your mind and heart on God, who loves you and will guide you. Although you like to hang out with friends and family, personal time is an important part of self-care. Allow yourself to meditate on the Bible passages on page 30—or choose your own favorites. God uses the Scripture you've committed to memory to do great work in you. You'll see. It will require a break from Snapchat and Instagram, but it'll be worth it. You're a girl who deserves to let peace and love sink into your mental space.

This chapter has allowed you to consider *who and whose you are*. Who are you? You're a beautifully created child of God. Whose are you? You are God's. You're a daughter of the Most High God. You've been redeemed in Christ, meaning your faith in Jesus makes you incredibly valuable. Confidently speak positivity over your life, even if it seems nobody else speaks it over you. You're working toward owning your Christian identity. Choose to share your faith and love for Jesus with less concern about what others might think. Be proud of who you are and show God's character in the way you treat others, even your enemies. If God is for you, then who can be against you (Romans 8:31)? Most of all, don't allow *you* to be against you. It's your time.

Chapter 3

My Safe Haven

You are my mighty rock, my fortress, my protector, the rock where I am safe, my shield, my powerful weapon, and my place of shelter. (Psalm 18:2, CEV)

God is your eternal spiritual home, your fortress, and your safe haven, always open to you and accessible wherever you go.

MY HOME IS IN GOD

Home has a spiritual meaning. Yearnings related to home have often been explored by Christian thought leaders as the pull of the soul. We all have an innate desire to draw near to God. When we feel lonely—even around what's familiar—it is a sure sign that we are longing for a greater connection with God, our true home. Life is a spiritual journey, and our ultimate home is in God, where love is unconditional. Just like the great feeling you might get when you close the door to your room after a long day, throw on your ugliest, comfiest lounge clothes, and plop across your bed with your go-to snack (fries and mayo, anyone?), in God you are safe to relax and let your true self shine. God already knows and loves you inside and out.

Tough Choices at Home

Even the best home life situations sometimes involve difficult choices. Check out this passage that shows how Jesus experienced this as he was entering his teen years:

Every year Jesus' parents traveled to Jerusalem for the Feast of Passover. When he was twelve years old, they went up as they always did for the Feast. When it was over and they left for home, the child Jesus stayed behind in Jerusalem, but his parents didn't know it. Thinking he was somewhere in the company of pilgrims, they journeyed for a whole day and then began looking for him among relatives and neighbors. When they didn't find him, they went back to Jerusalem looking for him.

The next day they found him in the Temple seated among the teachers, listening to them and asking questions. The teachers were all quite taken with him, impressed with the sharpness of his answers. But his parents were not impressed; they were upset and hurt.

His mother said, "Young man, why have you done this to us? Your father and I have been half out of our minds looking for you."

He said, "Why were you looking for me? Didn't you know that I had to be here, dealing with the things of my Father?" But they had no idea what he was talking about.

So he went back to Nazareth with them, and lived obediently with them. His mother held these things dearly, deep within herself. And Jesus matured, growing up in both body and spirit, blessed by both God and people. (Luke 2:41–52, MSG)

Even Jesus—perhaps feeling misunderstood and maybe angry that he wasn't given enough freedom—had to face choices about back talk and accepting parental boundaries.

Everyone at one point or another feels restless or discontent with their home situation, no matter the address or who else lives there. Whether that home has two loving parents, one who's almost never there, an aunt, a grandparent, or a guardian, no home perfectly satisfies. Cooperation, respectful speech, and backing down even when we know we're right are godly choices.

Jesus was God on earth, yet he put even that aside to accommodate his parents. When our spiritual home is in God, we can make godly choices, even when others at home get angry or frustrated with us or seem to have lost sight of who we are.

> My people will live in peaceful dwelling places,
> in secure homes, in undisturbed places of rest.
> (Isaiah 32:18, NIV)

Rest in the comfort of being at home with God in your spirit. He will give you peace wherever you are and no matter what your physical home environment is like.

Family Exercise

This exercise will help you consider your role in your family, how it makes you feel about yourself, and how that can impact your decisions. Check whether each statement is never true, sometimes true, usually true, or always true.

	NEVER	SOMETIMES	USUALLY	ALWAYS
I feel I am like the other members of my family.	☐	☐	☐	☐
I feel proud of my family.	☐	☐	☐	☐
I feel seen as who I really am by my family.	☐	☐	☐	☐
I feel comfortable bringing friends home.	☐	☐	☐	☐
My family does a good job with what's most important for families to do.	☐	☐	☐	☐
I'm good enough for my family.	☐	☐	☐	☐
I fit well into my family.	☐	☐	☐	☐
My family makes me feel worthy as a person.	☐	☐	☐	☐

	NEVER	SOMETIMES	USUALLY	ALWAYS
I feel comfortable in different family situations.	☐	☐	☐	☐
I play an important role in my family.	☐	☐	☐	☐
I am meeting the expectations my family has for me.	☐	☐	☐	☐
Among my friends' families, mine is just as good.	☐	☐	☐	☐

If you checked "never" or "sometimes" more than once, you're like most people. If you placed the most checks by "never," it's a good idea to consider how your feelings toward your family could influence your choices and behaviors. If you placed the most checks by "always," just make sure that you're letting the real you shine through and that you're nurturing your own special identity, apart from others in your family. Consider your responses to this exercise as you work through this chapter.

Now, challenge yourself to make this affirmation: "When I realize that my number one relationship is with God and that wherever I am, God is with me, I am home. Then, there truly is no place like home. Whether or not my physical home is filled with enough love and other things I need, I choose to be a godly presence there. The choices I make at home reveal the real me. How I interact with my family members is an important way that I grow in God."

Family Exercise: GOD'S POINT OF VIEW

Consider each statement and check whether it is never true, sometimes true, usually true, or always true from God's point of view. Then look up the Scripture verse that correlates with each statement.

	NEVER	SOMETIMES	USUALLY	ALWAYS
God feels I am like the other members of my family. [a]	☐	☐	☐	☐
God is proud of my family. [b]	☐	☐	☐	☐
Both God and my family see me for who I really am. [c]	☐	☐	☐	☐
God is pleased when I bring friends home. [d]	☐	☐	☐	☐
By God's standards, my family does a good job with what's most important for families to do. [e]	☐	☐	☐	☐
I'm good enough for my family, according to God's standards. [f]	☐	☐	☐	☐
God feels I fit well into my family. [g]	☐	☐	☐	☐
My relationship with God makes me feel worthy as a person. [h]	☐	☐	☐	☐
God is comfortable amidst my family's different situations. [i]	☐	☐	☐	☐

	NEVER	SOMETIMES	USUALLY	ALWAYS
God plays an important role in my family. [j]	☐	☐	☐	☐
I am meeting the expectations God has of me in my family. [k]	☐	☐	☐	☐
Among my friends' families, I feel God sees mine is just as good. [l]	☐	☐	☐	☐

a. Galatians 3:28 (ESV)

b. Ephesians 2:8 (NIV)

c. Psalm 139:1 (NIV)

d. 1 Peter 4:9 (NASB)

e. Ephesians 6:1–4 (CEV)

f. Romans 3:23–24 (CEV)

g. Colossians 3:13 (NIV)

h. Psalm 139:13–15 (NIV)

i. 1 Kings 8:27 (NASB)

j. Matthew 7:24–27 (NIV)

k. Romans 8:38–39 (ESV)

l. Romans 2:11 (NIV)

What personal changes will you make after considering how God views you and your family and after reading these Scriptures?

_____

_____

_____

Hopefully, this exercise helps you maintain healthy perspective on your home life and your role in your family. Remember, your choices about how to respond to your environment are opportunities to share God's transformative love with others.

The heavens are yours, and yours also the earth; you founded the world and all that is in it. (Psalm 89:11, NIV)

God—the Creator of the universe—made all space, beings, and things that exist in the earthly and heavenly realms. Amidst all of this spiritual and physical creation, you fit perfectly at home, just as you are.

HOLY MATH

No two families are the same. Some will struggle financially more than others, but maybe they're happy. Some have all the material wealth they could hope for but are not content. Some are both spiritually and monetarily depleted. Others seem pretty balanced. All families come with their positives and negatives and have or lack something. Whatever the case for your family, remember how much you *always have* with God. With God, you have everything. Without God, even if you're set up financially, you have nothing. It's like simple, holy math: **God + Nothing = Everything**. Being in Christ is all you need to have everything.

Holy Math Exercise: ADDITION

This exercise will challenge you to add more godly choices to your life and become more deeply at home in God's presence through your daily activities. Psalm 118:24 (NKJV) says, "This *is* the day the Lord has made." Each day already belongs to God, so let the Lord be present in a bigger way. Add God to your day, and it will impact you and your surroundings at home.

The following exercise will take you through a normal day, but to it you'll add variables like time for prayer, Scripture reading, encouragement to yourself, and telling someone else about Jesus. You will also set specific goals and action steps toward reaching your goals and for spiritual growth. I'll give you a few samples, but the rest of the brainstorming is up to you. As you work through this exercise, consider the goals and action steps that might positively impact your life at home among family.

Sample Exercises

God + School = Making friends, getting good grades, and earning awards.

Goal: To connect with new people and make the honor roll.

Action step: Try a new study group of friends on the honor roll and spend extra time working on assignments.

God + Prayer = Peace, love, joy, and concern for others by praying for them, too.

Goal: To become more positive and content, and to think about the needs of others.

Action steps: Designate daily prayer time; ask others what I can take to God on their behalf.

God + Me = _____.

Goal: _____.

Action step: _____.

God + Friends = _____.

Goal: _____.

Action step: _____.

God + Salvation = _____.

Goal: _____.

Action step: _____.

God + _____ = _____.

Goal: _____.

Action step: _____.

God + _____ = _____.

Goal: _____.

Action step: _____.

God + _____ = _____.

Goal: _____.

Action step: _____.

Once you are done, ask yourself, "How have I benefited from this exercise?" Journal your thoughts in the space provided. Then, over the next few months, use your action steps as a roadmap for reaching your goals. Revisit this exercise and see how you've done, how your choices have impacted your home life, or how you might adjust your plans.

_____

_____

_____

_____

_____

_____

_____

_____

This is love: not that we loved God, but that he loved us and sent his Son as an atoning sacrifice for our sins. (1 John 4:10, NIV)

God created love and *is* love. God's love is a gift freely given to us, not because of what we do. It is not earned. With people, it might seem as though the love of friends, guy friends, or even family is conditional and based on how you act, how you perform, or what your relationship does for them. We're all human, and nobody will perfectly please another. Try not to feel burdened under the pressure to earn someone's love, especially at home. That's not how God designed love. Instead, consider the difference between the way people love and how God loves. Try to express God's kind of love even when you don't think you're receiving it from friends or family. God will always be there for you.

Clearing Some Things Away to Get Closer to Home

God is love ... (1 John 4:8, CEV)

Because God's love and presence are so important in your life—your relationship with God is your spiritual home—it's good to make choices that nurture your connection with God. This exercise will help you replace any not-so-great choices or behaviors that might keep you from being closer to Jesus. Meanwhile, as you consider behaviors, you might also "toss out" some actions that are causing any issues for you in your physical home.

Materials needed:

* Scissors
* Paper or index cards
* A pen or a marker
* A trash can

Using a separate sheet of paper or index card for each one, write down some choices that you think might be holding you back from your best connection with your Creator. Is it lack of prayer or Bible study? Could it be taking sides in a family drama? What about joining in gossip about a family member or friend, instead of trying to help them? You know what it is! Write it down. Then, physically cut each card or piece of paper into the smallest pieces you can and throw them into the trash. You might also take the trash out after this exercise to get this negativity as far away from you as possible.

You could also have a sibling or other family member join you in doing this exercise so that you can hold each other accountable. Pray for God to show you the person who will take this journey with you. Then, come together in a couple of weeks to discuss how you've done with your choices and any improvement you are experiencing.

Do not be anxious *or* worried about anything, but in everything [every circumstance and situation] by prayer and petition with thanksgiving, continue to make your [specific] requests known to God.
(Philippians 4:6, AMP)

Your loving Lord doesn't want you to suffer worry or anxiety, which causes unhappiness and affects your choices. Your particular issues matter to God. You can take them all to God in prayer.

My Prayer Life: A DAILY FOUR-STEP PLAN

The practice of prayer is covered so much in this workbook. It's intentional! That's because prayer is more powerful and more available than any other tool you have to help you make good decisions. Rather than approaching prayer as a routine you only do during bad times or to bless your food, start treating it as something much bigger than that. Prayer is not a chore; it is a lifestyle. Prayer leads to good choices and a closer relationship with God. When you fuel your relationship with God through prayer, it transforms your mind, making it strong and best prepared for making decisions that contribute to a peaceful home and successful future.

For the next 21 days, try this four-step prayer plan to develop a lifestyle of prayer:

1. Pray in the morning as soon as you open your eyes, thanking God for waking you up. (Hey, it's a miracle that I even hear the alarm!)

2. Then, pray during a moment of silence at school, asking God to order your day and be present in the events and choices you face.

3. Pray after school, thanking God for keeping you safe and for any other blessings of the day.

4. Lastly, choose your own time to pray for someone else—a friend, a teacher, a family member, etc. Bonus: God encourages us to care for those closest to us (1 Timothy 5:8). Perhaps a relative in your home needs your prayers.

	WAKING	MOMENT OF SILENCE AT SCHOOL	AFTER SCHOOL	MY TIME/PRAYER FOR SOMEONE ELSE
1.				
2.				

	WAKING	MOMENT OF SILENCE AT SCHOOL	AFTER SCHOOL	MY TIME/PRAYER FOR SOMEONE ELSE
3.				
4.				
5.				
6.				
7.				
8.				
9.				
10.				
11.				
12.				
13.				

	WAKING	MOMENT OF SILENCE AT SCHOOL	AFTER SCHOOL	MY TIME/PRAYER FOR SOMEONE ELSE
14.				
15.				
16.				
17.				
18.				
19.				
20.				
21.				

While you add these new prayers to your life, don't forget to continue blessing your food or praying at night—whatever usual prayers you're already doing.

Keep track of your progress by journaling about it and making this a concrete plan. By the 21st day, you will have begun creating a powerful lifestyle of prayer.

When you consider who God is to you, many things might come to mind: provider, protector, giver of justice, supporter (Psalm 146:7–9). God is, of course, your Creator and an eternal force (Isaiah 40:28). Jesus is the way, the truth, and the life (John 14:6). But God is so much more than we can ever express! And at the center of all, God is love. Love.

Who Is God to Me?

Take some time to examine what you believe and how you feel about God's role in your life as you respond to the statements below. Circle "True" or "False" for each of the following statements.

God is my comfort in times of need.   **True / False**

God has forgotten me.   **True / False**

The Creator puts me first.   **True / False**

God answers my prayers.   **True / False**

God is a fixer.   **True / False**

God does not love me.   **True / False**

God never leaves me.   **True / False**

God is love during my time of need.   **True / False**

I'd rather listen to my parents than listen to God.   **True / False**

I do not like being on God's time.   **True / False**

God wants to control all of my life.   **True / False**

I am my own provider.   **True / False**

God is my spiritual home.   **True / False**

Are you feeling God-centered or spiritually distant? If you have any concerns or question your feelings about your answers, it's okay! Faith is a journey. Questions are inevitable and good. Talk to a trusted youth pastor, friend, or family member. Look for answers by spending some time with the Bible.

> But the Holy Spirit will come upon you and give you power. Then you will tell everyone about me ... everywhere in the world. (Acts 1:8, CEV)

Sharing Is Caring

As believers, we're called to share the wonderful truth of God's love with others.

It can be hard to speak up about your faith. Not everyone is open to hearing about it. You might not want to be challenged, or you may not know what to say. Still, it's an important part of your role as a follower of Jesus. Christ's love is meant to be shared. Whether you're the only believer in your family or one of many, try to embrace your opportunities to represent Christ. Share your faith. Spread the good news to every corner of your life, starting at home. Here's an exercise to get you sharing.

Ask God for guidance in whom you should approach to share your faith. Make a list on the lines provided. These are the people you'll introduce to the Creator of everything. After each name on the list, write a brief plan for how you'll approach them (the example provided is a suggested guide; individualize your plans!).

Name: *I'll text this person and ask them if they have any prayer requests. Then, I'll ask them if it is okay for me to call and pray with them.*

_____ : _____ .

_____ : _____ .

_____ : _____ .

_____ : _____ .

_____ : _____ .

Commit yourself to regularly checking in with each person on your list. You could have a life-changing impact on others. Stay focused. Remember that you're not in a race and no time is wasted when you're working for the Lord.

TO SUM UP

No matter what your home situation is—whether it's just okay, really awesome, or often a struggle—knowing that you are always at home in the Lord will help you make godly choices and represent God's love to those you live with. You belong to Jesus and can always feel at home in the Lord. Keeping in close contact with God through prayer will help you navigate home life situations. Jesus cherishes and wants to stay connected with you. Allow yourself to take refuge in this loving bond. Stay connected to Jesus.

Find happiness in sharing your safe haven with others. The amazing things you feel as a child of God are meant to be shared with those around you, so they, too, may feel a sense of belonging, comfort, peace, and joy. Tell others about what Christ means to you. Stay connected to God through prayer. Be uplifted, be secure at home, and claim your place under the wings of your caring Creator (Psalm 91:4).

Chapter 4

It's More Than Just School

Don't let anyone make fun of you, just because you are young. Set an example for other followers by what you say and do, as well as by your love, faith, and purity. (1 Timothy 4:12, CEV)

In other words, don't let others judge you for being young. Instead, set a positive example with your choices.

SCHOOL CAN BE A PLACE OF LOUD OPINIONS

You might think it's hard to be a representative of Christ at school. Don't underestimate your potential. Remember young David, who took down the giant, Goliath (1 Samuel 17). That battle seemed impossible for someone of his age and size, especially compared with his enemy. I'm sure you've heard the story many times, but it's worth revisiting as a reminder that God can use anyone and everyone. You can shine for God, no matter if you're young or old or whether or not you feel *big* enough to do significant things. School, church, social, and family situations are all opportunities for you to do great work. You don't have to knock down a bully, but God will give you opportunities to lead others through your choices and actions. In this chapter, we'll tackle some of the issues you might face at school and how to overcome them.

> If God is on our side, can anyone be against us?
> (Romans 8:31, CEV)

God's opinion of you is more important than that of any friend or foe. God is always for you, even when others aren't. Nothing can change God's unwavering devotion to you.

HOW IMPORTANT ARE OTHERS' OPINIONS OF ME?

In high school, being liked or popular might seem like a big deal. But the truth is, those who are popular in high school are not necessarily popular after graduation—especially if they did a lot of goofing off to impress people and fell short in their studies. A more important goal than being liked or popular is developing the strength to act according to your faith.

Knowing that God is for you and has your back can make it easier to honor God with your choices. Your Lord is not concerned with how many likes you get when you post on Instagram, and although it feels nice to get some love on Instagram, it's not worth worrying too much about. You don't want to waste precious time trying to win the approval of others, especially those whose approval is fickle or who require you to act against your beliefs. True friends will love and accept you for who you are. The quality of a friendship is more important than the quantity of friends. Popularity is not a measure of what God can do through you or what kind of opportunities you'll have. God loves to do amazing things through people who surprise the world!

An Unlikely Leader

The Bible tells of a woman named Deborah who lived at a time when women had very few rights and men ruled. Yet she was a prophet and judge, and God even sent her into battle for her people.

Deborah was a prophet, the wife of Lappidoth. She was judge over Israel at that time. She held court under Deborah's Palm between Ramah and Bethel in the hills of Ephraim. The People of Israel went to her in matters of justice.

She sent for Barak son of Abinoam from Kedesh in Naphtali and said to him, "It has become clear that God, the God of Israel, commands you: Go to Mount Tabor and prepare for battle. Take ten companies of soldiers from Naphtali and Zebulun. I'll take care of getting Sisera, the leader of Jabin's army, to the Kishon River with all his chariots and troops. And I'll make sure you win the battle."

Barak said, "If you go with me, I'll go. But if you don't go with me, I won't go."

She said, "Of course I'll go with you. But understand that with an attitude like that, there'll be no glory in it for you. God will use a woman's hand to take care of Sisera." (Judges 4:4–10, MSG).

How amazing it must have been, in an era when women were not heard, that Deborah was a leader who spoke into the important matters of her community. God placed Deborah in position to fulfill a wonderful purpose, and she accepted the work as a privilege. She knew it was best to be true to her faith above anything else. And, in response to her bravery, God opened doors for her. The Almighty will do the same for you, too!

Prayer of Security in Who I Am

Read this prayer when you need to be affirmed in who you are and for strength when you don't feel accepted by others.

Dear Savior,

My life is centered on you. My steps are directed by you. You are for me. Who can be against me? I will not be broken by negativity from anyone. You are able to bless me and my family. I know that because I am yours, I am more than a conqueror. Because you created me, I am special. Please help me wear my faith proudly. I am here for your purpose and to glorify your name. Amen.

Reflection Questions

Take a moment to think about how God is working in your school life, and note your thoughts about the following questions in the spaces provided.

In what ways have you felt limited by the judgments or stereotypes others put upon you?

_____

_____

What are some situations where you struggle to express your faith? (Or do you truly own your faith at school? Why?)

_____

_____

What are some areas in your life that are calling you to step up? How will you do it?

_____

_____

With God's power to remove limitations, what would you most want to do? Pray about it and make it so!

_____

_____

Take a moment to reflect on these questions and your responses to them. Maybe you are holding back a little, and all you need is some more time in prayer to get the courage you need to step into the role God has for you at school.

Do I Represent God at School?

This exercise will allow you to assess whether you are representing your awesome Creator to your peers. Answer by placing a check mark in either the "Yes" or "No" boxes below.

	YES	NO
Do I use profanity?	☐	☐
Do I fight at school?	☐	☐
Do I pick on anyone because of how they dress, their skill levels, or any other reason?	☐	☐
Do I help others who are being bullied?	☐	☐
Do I present a Christlike character?	☐	☐
Have I ever talked back to my teachers?	☐	☐
Am I disrespectful?	☐	☐
Am I friendly to others?	☐	☐
Do I help my teachers in class?	☐	☐
Do I encourage others?	☐	☐
Do I share with others?	☐	☐
Do I talk negatively behind other students' backs?	☐	☐

Consider your answers to this assessment and whether you have anything to work on. Feel free to take the quiz again in a month. Remember: It is never too late to start making better choices.

God cares for you, so turn all your worries over to him. (1 Peter 5:7, CEV)

I Will Never Get Over . . .

In the Lord, you have safe and caring support for your inner struggles. High school can feel like the Colosseum from the movie *Gladiator* at times. Because that movie is probably too old a reference for your generation (bonus points if you know it), let me explain: In high school, it's like an arena where opponents are ready to pounce on any mistake or embarrassing thing that happens . . . and the crowd, thirsty for entertainment, goes wild!

Maybe you've had an utterly embarrassing moment at school. Maybe you've been publicly mistreated by a guy or girl, and it feels like the whole school is talking about you. Or maybe you are carrying a secret burden, something that has happened that you're having trouble letting go of. Let's turn it over to God, right now! In the blank space, write in the thing that's bugging you or the experience you've decided to keep pushing below the surface.

I will never get over _____.

Now, write your name on the line that appears in the Scripture verse below.

God cares for me, _____**, so I will turn all my worries over to God (1 Peter 5:7).**

Read the sentence above out loud.

Trust God's power to heal your heart now that you've begun to let go of this burden. If you feel twinges of pain about it again, repeat the verse with your name. I also encourage you to talk with a trusted adult about any feelings that are bringing you down. The Bible stresses the importance of encouraging and spending time with one another.

Let us be concerned for one another, to help one another to show love and to do good. Let us not give up the habit of meeting together. . . . Instead, let us encourage one another all the more, since you see that the Day of the Lord is coming nearer.

(Hebrews 10:24–25, GNT)

My Likes and Dislikes about School

Finding your people—those who accept you and have some similar likes and whose company you enjoy—is a wonderful way to experience high school, life, and your faith journey.

Take a look at the list below and select "Like" or "Dislike" to help make your interests clearer:

Homework or studying	**Like / Dislike**
Hanging out in a large group of peers	**Like / Dislike**
Cooking	**Like / Dislike**
Working out	**Like / Dislike**
Playing sports	**Like / Dislike**
Listening to music	**Like / Dislike**
Making music	**Like / Dislike**
Reading books	**Like / Dislike**
Dancing	**Like / Dislike**
Prayer	**Like / Dislike**
Volunteering	**Like / Dislike**

If you're struggling to find your crew, one place to start is shared interests. Perhaps there's a prayer group, study group, drama club, book club, cooking club, or sports club you could get involved in—or even launch—to meet some new friends. Maybe you'll start a band or meet some people by volunteering. Pray about it, and God will guide you to your people!

My Mentors

The best example of mentorship is in the Bible. God calls his people to be mentors—to lovingly and generously look over and serve those in their care. He also urges those who are being guided to respect authority and be humble.

Church leaders, I am writing to encourage you. I too am a leader, as well as a witness to Christ's suffering, and I will share in his glory when it is shown to us.

Just as shepherds watch over their sheep, you must watch over everyone God has placed in your care. Do it willingly in order to please God, and not simply because you think you must. Let it be something you want to do, instead of something you do merely to make money. Don't be bossy to those people who are in your care, but set an example for them. Then when Christ the Chief Shepherd returns, you will be given a crown that will never lose its glory.

All of you young people should obey your elders. In fact, everyone should be humble toward everyone else. The Scriptures say, "God opposes proud people, but he helps everyone who is humble." (1 Peter 5:1–5, CEV)

Think about the people who have the most positive impact on your life. Usually, a mentor is older, but they can be your age if that's true for you. Make a list in the space provided, naming these people and what their guidance and time mean to you.

_____

_____

_____

_____

Remaining humble as you are guided by a mentor is a godly choice. To show your gratitude to your mentor, consider writing a brief note of thanks to them for how they help you. Use the space provided to draft it, and then copy it onto a note card to give to your mentor.

_____

_____

_____

_____

_____

And though your beginning was small, your latter days will be very great. (Job 8:7, ESV)

With mentorship, where you find yourself now will not compare to the great things in store for your future.

Journal Entry: HIGH SCHOOL IS LIKE . . .

This exercise allows you to reflect on and write about your life at school. No need to worry about structure—just write your thoughts about your high school experience, how it makes you feel, and what it means. If you run out of room and want to keep writing, use a journal or spare sheet of paper.

_____

_____

_____

_____

_____

Revisit this journal entry at the end of your semester or school year. How have your feelings changed or stayed the same? Have you taken opportunities to be a light for God's love among your peers? What decisions would you change? What was the biggest lesson you learned in school this year?

_____

_____

_____

_____

_____

_____

_____

"I WISH I COULD CHANGE MY HAIR, SKIN, FACE, OR BODY."

Such thoughts can make you second-guess your whole existence. You live in the age of constant comparison, when people will go to great lengths to adjust their appearance for acceptance and the perfect online image. Choose not to compare yourself with so-called beauty ideals you see on the Internet, in magazines, on television, or at school. You were made in the likeness of God; everything about you is special. You are already an ideal beauty—you're God's wonderful creation. The Creator didn't intend for the creation—you—to "fix" God's masterful work. And your body is made to do a lot more than look pretty. Choose to act in a way that reflects love for your body and who you are. There's nothing more beautiful than the confidence that comes from knowing you are a loved and wonderful creation of God.

> So God created human beings, making them to be like himself. He created them male and female.
> (Genesis 1:27, GNT)

Daily Self-Love

For a confidence boost, recite the following motivational phrases in front of your mirror every morning.

I am beautiful.	*I am focused.*	*I am me. So let it be.*
I am loved.	*I am strong.*	*I am a child of God.*
I am educated.	*I am awesome.*	

Continue this practice and see how it impacts the course of your day. Share this exercise with a friend who needs it. Take her to a mirror and have her say these lines out loud. Sharing the love of God to help boost a friend's confidence will be a wonderful gift to you both.

My Plan for Success in School

Commit your work to the Lord, and your plans will be established. (Proverbs 16:3, ESV)

In other words, be faithful to God, who blesses and ensures your plans. Commit to the following statements by reading them aloud as a proclamation over your school year:

I will not procrastinate.

I will prioritize my homework to ensure it's done on time.

I will ask for help or tutoring if I need it.

I will never give in or give up.

I will inform my teacher of any distractions from other students.

I will humbly talk to my teachers if I feel misunderstood by them.

I will aim for As and Bs, but I will not be angry with myself if I get a C.

I will try hard in all of my subjects.

I will not hang out with friends if I have homework or a project due.

I will make my phone less of a priority.

Revisit this plan at the end of the year. How many commitments were you able to keep? Make these proclamations again at the start of each subsequent year in high school. You are capable of upholding these plans, which will make for a successful and fulfilling school experience.

TO SUM UP

As a believer, you are called to share the love of God wherever you go; that includes school, which can sometimes be challenging. Even at your young age, you have the power to represent God's love to others by making godly decisions. Your good choices will not only positively impact others but also set you up for a bright future. You are never too young to lead, and God uses even the most unexpected people to do great work. Be a godly example among your peers.

Find your people. Love yourself as God loves you. Establish a strong plan for a great school experience. Pray that your school is a place where you can connect with friends who support you and whom you support in faith. You are an amazing young lady. Blessings on all you do!

Spiritual growth is expressed in more ways than in words. Use this page to express yourself by coloring, drawing, doodling or other graphics.

Chapter 5

True Friendship 101

One who has unreliable friends soon comes to ruin,
but there is a friend who sticks closer than a brother.
(Proverbs 18:24, NIV)

The Bible is a great place to learn about true friendship—a bond that
can grow and last forever. Such friendships are built on honesty, faith,
loyalty, and, most of all, love. God wants us to have friends but,
especially, to find a friend in Jesus.

IN THESE DAYS OF SOCIAL MEDIA, ONLINE FRIENDSHIPS ARE CONSIDERED NORMAL

They are launched quickly, sometimes on impulse, and it also only takes a millisecond to end a Snapchat friendship. True friendship is about more than *likes* and *dislikes*. It is more than shares and emojis. We are generally quick to instant message or tweet new friends, but for a friendship to maintain its value over time, friends will need to exhibit loyalty, love, compassion, sympathy, and honesty; they'll also need to be able to keep their relationship drama-free. It's a lot of effort to foster friendship IRL, and these friendships require time in person, good communication, and being there for each other when it matters most. Choose to invest your time in friendships that have a future with people who will enhance your spiritual life. It's fun and easy to get swept up in the quasi-fantasy world of social media friending, but don't miss out on true quality bonds with people who are as committed to the relationship as you are.

Also, our social-media-only friendships can lack true depth, which is hard to establish if your relationship is low commitment, as online relationships tend to be. Sure, you might like a comment here or there, or indulge your curiosity by keeping up with what your cyber pals are doing. But it's more important to say "Hi!" or ask "How are you doing?" with genuine concern when you see friends in the hallways at school. Making great decisions about how you interact with others means your online and in-person activities align. If you engage someone online, don't ignore them in person. Or perhaps you should declutter your friends list, leaving only those with whom you truly share of yourself. True friendship is about good communication. And when you open your heart to each other in real time spent together, it will only strengthen your bond.

> Walk with the wise and become wise, for a companion of fools suffers harm. (Proverbs 13:20, NIV)

In other words, the kind of people you choose to be around matters; your friends will influence your actions, whether wise or foolish.

Social Media Blackout

As you decide which friendships to focus on, invite one of those friends to try this exercise with you. It's time to bring back face-to-face interactions (and I don't mean FaceTime). We need real, in-person interactions to strengthen our friendships. This requires you to do something everyone hates to do: unplug. When you and your friend spend time together, commit to shutting off any devices on which you might be tempted to check social media. (When you shut down, be sure to only log out of your social media accounts and not physically power off your cell phone. You should still have access to any important phone calls.) This will put you more deeply in tune with one another and let you experience fully being in the moment. It will also remove the distracting urge to check what other teens you both know are doing on social media, so your time can be spent on each other. I hope, through this exercise, you sense the joy of choosing to be present with your friend. There really is nothing like it!

Plan a Girl Outing and Write about It

Plan a girl outing and, again, spend time with your friend without using social media. Use the outing to reconnect with each other and build up your friendship. Whether you go out to dinner or walk around the mall, spend this time enjoying each other's company without distraction. Also, try to avoid using this friend time to scope out guys. There is power in numbers, and time with a friend might seem like the right time to approach a guy, but your outing is about you and your friend. Giving that friend your undivided attention is a good choice.

Once you've had your outing, both of you journal about the experience. Then, set a time when you'll read your journal entries to each other. This, again, sparks more face-to-face interactions.

You

_____

_____

_____

_____

_____

Your friend

_____

_____

_____

_____

_____

A friend loves at all times, and a [sister] is born for
a time of adversity. (Proverbs 17:17, NIV)

The Bible describes a friend as someone who loves you through everything. The closest of
friends—those whose actions make them feel like blood relatives—will help you through
your greatest struggles.

DEFINING MOMENTS OF A TRUE FRIENDSHIP

True friendships are defined when you or your friend experience a major, or life-altering, situation. Did she comfort you during a breakup? Were you there for her when her parents divorced? Was she there for you when you lost a family member? The way each of you responds to the other's adversity defines your friendship. It's always a good choice to be a friend and care for someone in need. But if you're not on the receiving end of that kind of care from your friends, it might be time to seek out some new ones.

Finding True Friendship

Use the following questions to identify the true friends in your life. Name someone who was with you in each of the situations that are relevant to you.

_____ *comforted me during a breakup.*

_____ *was there for me when my parents divorced.*

_____ *was there for me when I lost a family member.*

_____ *has kept all my secrets.*

_____ *has been loyal to me.*

We are better when we have people around us who exhibit love, loyalty, compassion, trust, and sympathy. Remember to make decisions that help *you* uphold the same *true friend* characteristics. It's best to avoid a one-sided friendship.

I comforted _____ *during a breakup.*

I was there for _____ *when her parents divorced.*

*I was there for*_____ *when she lost a family member.*

I have kept all _____ *'s secrets.*

I have been loyal to _____.

QUALITY OUTRANKS QUANTITY WHEN IT COMES TO TRUE FRIENDSHIP

This exercise will help you choose whether you want to be known as the one with the most friends or the one with the truest friend. The following questions will allow you to evaluate what you value most in a friendship. Check "yes" or "no" in the spaces provided.

	YES	NO
I prefer to travel in groups.	☐	☐
I need several people's opinions.	☐	☐
I tend to bring everyone into a group text.	☐	☐
I get mad when only one friend likes my post.	☐	☐
I get mad when only one friend responds to my group text message.	☐	☐
I cancel on my friends and wonder why they get upset.	☐	☐

If you answered "yes" to two or more of these questions, consider ways to engage friends that honor quality instead of quantity.

Be open and honest with yourself as you check "yes" or "no" in the spaces provided.

	YES	NO
I prefer to travel with one person.	☐	☐
I need just one friend's opinion.	☐	☐
I tend to relate to my friends individually.	☐	☐
I feel disappointed when a friend cancels on me.	☐	☐

Within the next couple of weeks, challenge yourself to make some minor changes in your friendships based on your results.

BRICKS THAT BUILD FRIENDSHIPS

Three things will last forever—faith, hope,
and love—and the greatest of these is love.
(1 Corinthians 13:13, NLT)

The Bible often describes the importance of **love**. Of all the eternal powers in the universe, love is the greatest. That's why friendships should be built on love. Love is crucial to the structure of a lasting friendship.

Relationships are built brick by brick. Each brick carries a word on it. The brick that lays down the foundation and allows the friendship to be stable is called "love."

In friendship, love and loyalty go hand in hand. When you're building your friendship circle, you'll want to seek the loyal brick and *be* the loyal brick who firmly supports a friend, no matter the circumstance. Being loyal is a godly decision. Although a friend might be disloyal to you, it doesn't mean that you should be disloyal in return. Or perhaps a friend experiences a public embarrassment at school that kicks off a teasing ring. Whether you choose to ignore your friend's trouble or join in the jokes or stand up for your friend is important. God will reward you for following the way of Jesus Christ to stand up for your friend.

Most of us only have a few loyal brick friends in a lifetime. Choose your friends wisely and have their backs. And when a friend is disloyal to you, know that some people lack the spiritual guidance to be loyal. Continue to treat them with kindness and do to others as you would have them do to you (Luke 6:31).

My Loyal Brick Friends

This exercise allows you to visualize what you're looking for in friends. Think about your friends and write the names of those who are most loyal to you.

1. _____

2. _____

3. _____

The next brick in your friendship structure is **respect**. You want a friend who has deep appreciation for you, treats you with kindness, and doesn't want to offend. Your friend needs to understand your spiritual beliefs. It's good when you choose to be friends with those who share your spiritual beliefs. They, too, will understand the significance of these characteristics of friendship. Choosing friends who share your faith gives you an opportunity to show mutual respect and help each other on your most important journeys.

A friendship also needs to have a **trustworthy** brick. You should be able to rely on friends to be truthful and honest with you, no matter the circumstance. (Yes, I want to know if I have something green in my teeth!) You should be able to count on a friend to honor you whether you're together or in other company, and she should be able to trust you in the same way. There's nothing two-faced about true friendship!

The foundation of true friendship is solid and unshakable. Therefore, it takes time to build a friendship, to lay the bricks of a structure that will hopefully last your lifetime. God sees your heart and wants you to surround yourself with those who respect, love, and are loyal and truthful to you.

Show your brick friends that you value them with a phone call, a hug, or by doing something special for them. And, most important, be the kind of friend you're looking for.

I Am Respectful and Trustworthy. Are You?

This exercise is going to help you be a more respectful and trustworthy young lady of God. Also, it will encourage you to seek out friends who are respectful and trustworthy. The questions below will be answered with "Usually," "Sometimes," or "Not Often Enough."

1. I respect my friends.   **Usually / Sometimes / Not Often Enough**

2. I am polite to my friends.   **Usually / Sometimes / Not Often Enough**

3. I listen to my friends.   **Usually / Sometimes / Not Often Enough**

4. I'm a friend who is approachable.   **Usually / Sometimes / Not Often Enough**

5. I am a trustworthy friend.   **Usually / Sometimes / Not Often Enough**

6. I choose friends who are trustworthy.   **Usually / Sometimes / Not Often Enough**

7. My friends exhibit honest character.   **Usually / Sometimes / Not Often Enough**

8. My friends listen to me.   **Usually / Sometimes / Not Often Enough**

9. I am incorporating God in my friendship building.   **Usually / Sometimes / Not Often Enough**

If you have found yourself answering with "sometimes" in more than 50 percent of this exercise, consider what choices you can make to improve yourself and your friendships.

A FRIEND WHO LAYS A BRICK OF SYMPATHY IS A WINNER

> Our High Priest is not one who cannot feel sympathy for our weaknesses. On the contrary, we have a High Priest who was tempted in every way that we are . . .
> (Hebrews 4:15, GNT)

The Bible often describes the sympathy of Jesus. Christ sympathizes with your every struggle because he was tempted the same way as humans are. In our striving to live according to God's way, we should not forget to have sympathy for our friends. Making the godly decision to show care and understanding will go a long way toward securing a lifelong bond.

A true friend can sympathize with your struggles as if they are her own. The same goes for you in the role of sympathizer. To have a friend present with you in your time of need is like winning an award. In today's world, it seems many people are focused on their own pain, happiness, success, or gratification. It's an honor to give a friend your presence, concern, and time. When we choose to show sympathy to our friends, we reflect God's love, and our relationships grow to a higher purpose.

I Am Sympathetic

This exercise encourages you to look at your choices and identify when you have been a sympathetic friend. Complete each statement by sharing some ways you've shown sympathy for your friends. Having a sympathetic spirit allows you to focus less on yourself. Your unselfish decisions help you become the great young lady that God made you to be.

Example: I was sympathetic when I helped my friend get through her parents' divorce.

I was sympathetic when _____

I was sympathetic when _____

I was sympathetic when _____

I was sympathetic when _____

I was sympathetic when _____

I was sympathetic when _____

How do you feel since you have completed this assignment?

_____

_____

_____

_____

Do your choices reveal that you're a sympathetic friend?

_____

_____

_____

_____

We've been digging deep. Great work at answering honestly and being committed to the growth that's happening as you complete this workbook!

Self-Assessment to Be More Approachable: DO I . . . ?

Do not forsake your friend . . . (Proverbs 27:10, NIV)

The Bible shares the importance of being there for your friends—as someone who is attuned to their needs and can be counted on. This exercise encourages self-reflection that will help you be the best friend you can be. You will uncover how you treat others.

As you answer "Usually," "Sometimes," or "Not Often Enough," make sure to be honest with yourself, just as you're working toward being open and honest with your friends. If you sense that you have some negativity to work on, no problem! It might mean you make some very minor changes, like putting yourself out there with an invitation to your friends. But these changes are worth making, and they'll improve your friendships and your life.

I greet people with a smile.	**Usually / Sometimes / Not Often Enough**
I present my body language with open arms.	**Usually / Sometimes / Not Often Enough**
I sigh when someone is speaking to me.	**Usually / Sometimes / Not Often Enough**
I listen to respond rather than listen to understand.	**Usually / Sometimes / Not Often Enough**
I initiate outings with my friends rather than wait to be invited.	**Usually / Sometimes / Not Often Enough**
I check on my friend rather than wait for her to check on me.	**Usually / Sometimes / Not Often Enough**

Take this assessment further by asking a friend to evaluate your answers. Does she agree with your findings? Her feedback should allow you to make better choices to be more approachable, open, and dependable to your friends. Let her write her thoughts below.

Your friend

GIRL POWER

You will lose your friends if you keep talking about what they did wrong. (Proverbs 17:9, CEV)

Only God is meant to be a judge. We should never derive joy from tearing someone down or spreading awareness of their shortcomings. Too many things divide women in our culture, and we can tear each other down in too many ways. Make conscious decisions to uplift the ladies in your life. Women should look out for each other and offer help for the unique challenges we face. When someone criticizes a girlfriend, don't jump on the bandwagon. Let your actions speak sympathy and love.

Make a List of Girls You Are Going to Uplift Each Day for Seven Days and See How It Strengthens Your Friendship

Sunday _____

Monday _____

Tuesday _____

Wednesday _____

Thursday _____

Friday _____

Saturday _____

Once the week is over, ask each person you uplifted how she is feeling. This is a great opportunity to receive feedback from your friend or spark an ongoing trend of deeper communication and support.

Friend Appreciation Week

This challenge will inspire you with ways to encourage one specific friend. Start at the top of the week.

Day 1 (Sunday)

Text your friend to let her know how much you appreciate her.

Day 2 (Monday)

Send a direct message to your friend with a picture of the two of you. Tell her, "I love our friendship because . . ." (and, of course, fill in the reason you love your friendship).

Day 3 (Tuesday)

Send her a morning Snap. Just say, "Good morning (her name). I hope you have a good day!"

Day 4 (Wednesday)

WCW: Make this your Wednesday post on your social media. Post a picture of your friend for Women Crush Wednesday just to highlight your appreciation for her.

Day 5 (Thursday)

Tell your friend that it is Thankful Thursday and you're very thankful for your friendship.

Day 6 (Friday)

On this day, flash back to some of the fun times the two of you have had together. Send a flashback picture via text to your friend. This will show her that your friendship is enduring and that you cherish it.

Day 7 (Saturday)

This day should be called Saturday Bond Day. Just bonding and building. The two of you will go to your home and just play games, talk, dance, or have fun. This will end your Friend Appreciation Week.

You are made to have friends, and, as friends, you are to give each other strength. It is better to be in relationship with others than it is to be alone. Remember these Scripture passages as you make decisions to honor God in your friendships:

God has chosen you and made you his holy people. He loves you. So you should always clothe yourselves with mercy, kindness, humility, gentleness, and patience. Bear with each other, and forgive each other. If someone does wrong to you, forgive that person because the Lord forgave you. Even more than all this, clothe yourself in love. Love is what holds you all together in perfect unity. (Colossians 3:12–14, NCV)

Two people are better than one, because they get more done by working together. If one falls down, the other can help [her] up. But it is bad for the person who is alone and falls, because no one is there to help. (Ecclesiastes 4:9–10, NCV)

True Friendship Is a Feeling

Friendship should not be motivated by superficial things like social status, material benefit, or how it makes you appear to others. It's about how you make each other feel. First, ask yourself the following questions to see if you're choosing friendships based on the way your friendship looks to others or because of how it feels to you and your friend.

How do I feel once I have spent time with my friend?

_____

In what ways am I able to be myself (or not) around my friend?

_____

Am I embarrassed about my friend in certain circles, or is she embarrassed about me?

_____

Do I have to watch what I say around my friend, or am I able to be myself?

_____

Do I try to make friends I think can help me gain status?

_____

Do I try to make friends who live a more extravagant lifestyle than I do?

_____

Do I trust my friend around my boyfriend?

_____

These questions should help you determine whether your friendships are based on God's purpose for you in relationships. Once you have answered the questions, you might reevaluate some of the friendships in your life.

Acquaintance to Friend

A sweet friendship refreshes the soul.
(Proverbs 27:9, MSG)

In life, there is much to cause delight, but a great friendship is one of your most special spiritual treasures. The gift of friendship still has to be nurtured and grown. It takes time for an acquaintanceship to develop into a true friendship. It doesn't happen overnight.

The following questions will help you assess your potential new true friendship. Check "yes" or "no" below.

	YES	NO
Have they asked questions about you?	☐	☐
Do the conversations shift from surface to semi-deep things about them?	☐	☐
Are they usually engrossed in your conversations?	☐	☐
Do they initiate plans to meet up for more good times?	☐	☐
Do you find yourself telling them about your personal life?	☐	☐
Do you feel comfortable talking with them about your faith?	☐	☐

If you have answered "yes" to more than two of these questions, chances are you've chosen a great new friend. Speak with your acquaintance about your thoughts and see if they, too, think you mesh well together. Then see how the friendship develops.

Meeting Friends

Sometimes we're too nervous to approach potential friends in a store, at school, at church, at a game, or even at another friend's party. Here are some things to try that will push you out of your comfort zone and help you make new friends.

Start a conversation. If you're at school, bring up something you know you have in common, like an upcoming assignment, or ask about the other's weekend plans.

Try joining a new club at school. Look for groups whose interests align with yours, and also whose faith does, when possible. Sharing a passion for God with others is a great foundation for a friendship.

Unplug and interact IRL. While at your school's next sporting event, unplug from all social media and focus on interacting with the people there.

Introduce yourself. A simple "Hi. My name is _____" often works.

Try to make choices that set you up for good social interaction. Go out of your way to be friendly. Once you've become more relaxed, you will see that it's possible to make new friends.

I Am . . .

This exercise is all about building up self-confidence as a friend or potential friend. Your strengthened confidence is going to open new doors in your life. Speak your "I Ams" in the mirror for 21 days and use the following list to check off that you've recited your daily "I Ams."

I am approachable.	*I am focused.*	*I am caring.*
I am a true friend.	*I am loving.*	*I am compassionate.*
I am a child of God.	*I am genuine.*	*I am loyal.*
I am strong.	*I am honest.*	*I am sympathetic.*

1. ☐   4. ☐   7. ☐   10. ☐   13. ☐   16. ☐   19. ☐

2. ☐   5. ☐   8. ☐   11. ☐   14. ☐   17. ☐   20. ☐

3. ☐   6. ☐   9. ☐   12. ☐   15. ☐   18. ☐   21. ☐

Once the 21 days are up, journal about how this exercise has made you feel.

_____

_____

_____

_____

If choosing to say these affirmations has had a positive impact, feel free to continue saying them or any others that will reinforce your confidence each day.

TO SUM UP

God made you special. God honors true friendship. Our Lord never meant for us to live life alone. God does not want us to go through life lacking friends. Read the book of Ruth in the Bible for an illustration of how beautiful true friendship can be. Ruth and Naomi had each other to lean on through tragedy, and together they celebrated some very happy moments. Ruth exhibits all the true friendship characteristics. She was loyal and would not leave her friend Naomi who needed her. Ruth said: "Where you go I will go, and where you stay I will stay. Your people will be my people and your God my God" (Ruth 1:16, NIV). She showed love for Naomi by staying by her side. She was compassionate toward Naomi even though she had her own pain of loss. God wants us to be friendly. The friends God wants you to choose will be the ones who stick with you like family.

Spiritual growth is expressed in more ways than in words. Use this page to express yourself by coloring, drawing, doodling or other graphics.

Chapter 6

Friend Zone or Not?

And the scripture was fulfilled that says, "Abraham believed God, and it was credited to him as righteousness," and he was called God's friend.
(James 2:23 NIV)

Find Friendship in Jesus's Company

You are who you hang around.
In the midst of your sorrow, who do you hang around?
Do you hang around Jesus?

Do you hang around Mama?
Do you hang around Daddy?
Do you hang around that person who said you couldn't make it?
Do you hang around Jesus?

Are you stuck on what other people think?
Or are you stuck on Jesus?

You are who you hang around.
So hang around JESUS.

GOD—A DIVINE PRINCE

Love and dating are portrayed in our culture like a fairy tale, but they are actually hard to navigate, even when you and others have the best of intentions. The dating field is full of hurdles, especially as a teen. Intense feelings for someone can be a challenge to good decision-making. Desiring companionship and the touch of another might cause you to push the limits of your boundaries. You might find yourself being driven to please or trying to convince someone else of your worth. It can affect the way you dress, speak, or act.

God knows you'll face struggles. Your Creator knows your every movement and thought (Psalm 139:2). God loves you and will be there. Let God be your Divine Prince who will help you make wise choices about dating (or not dating). God will give you patience in your quest for love and be your refuge when things are less-than-fairytale-like.

Whether or not you're dating anyone right now, it's not too early to think about the characteristics that are most important to you in that person. You spend time with a variety of people every day. It's always possible to develop a crush or have feelings for someone. When it happens, you might tell yourself that you can influence the other person for good or accept them as they are. It might work for a time but not in the long run. God has given us clarity about whom we should align ourselves with. Only someone who understands your faith will be able to fully appreciate your boundaries and why they're important to you. And only by a personal choice does another person become dedicated to Christ.

Set an example of Christ's love and direction by following the Bible's guidance for relationships. Being intentional about the company you keep—friends and boyfriends—is not only a good choice, it's biblical. Let the power of your mind—not just your heart—take an active role in your dating decisions!

Friend Zone? . . . Or Is He Interested?

Above all else, guard your heart, for everything you do flows from it. (Proverbs 4:23, NIV)

The Bible makes clear the importance of protecting your heart. Setting clear standards and boundaries will help you protect your feelings, prevent you from being hurt, and, most of all, set you on a path to a fulfilling relationship at the right time in your life.

If you're not sure what to make of your situation, take spiritual control of all situations. Spend time in prayer. Stay close to God. Your Creator—who made you with feelings and urges and attractions—will hear your prayer and help you find the answers you need.

This exercise is also meant to help you get clarity. Circle the phrases that describe your relationship

1. He only hangs with me when we're in a group.

2. He enjoys spending time with just me.

3. He Snapchats me about his day.

4. He greets me with "good morning" and makes a point to message me "good night."

5. He is always talking about my friends and how good they look.

6. It's hard to keep his attention when we're together because he's always checking out other girls.

7. He tells me I'm pretty.

8. He asked me to hook him up with a girl at our school.

9. He says he does not want a relationship.

   "Friend Zone" statements are 1, 5, 6, 8, 9.

   "He's Interested" statements are 2, 3, 4, 7.

If you've circled two or more Friend Zone statements, chances are this guy is not ready to be your boyfriend, and that's a good thing. In this season of your life, do God's plans for you really include a boyfriend? Pray about it and seek the guidance of a pastor, parent, or friend if you need extra encouragement deciding to keep it in the Friend Zone.

Is He Just My Crush or More?

Sometimes it's hard to know if there's more to the crush you might have on one of your guy friends. If you're having trouble letting go of the possibility of something with him, welcome to the womanly world of crushes. Attractions are natural and don't at all mean we need to act on them. Think of crushes like birds flying in the air. We can appreciate their beauty and take breathless enjoyment watching them soar, but we don't want to let them nest in our hair.

This quiz will help you figure out if a crush is getting beyond the Friend Zone.

Circle "True" or "False":

We started hanging out in a group but now sometimes hang
out with just the two of us. **True / False**

We spend hours on the phone talking or texting. **True / False**

He told others that he likes me more than as a friend. **True / False**

He gives me "you look good" types of compliments. **True / False**

Your friends think that the two of you should be together. **True / False**

If you answer "True" to two or more of these questions, the crush is beyond the Friend Zone. You must set some boundaries.

MY STANDARDS AND BOUNDARIES

Crushes can escalate quickly, especially if you haven't really thought about your personal view on getting physical or talked with your crush about your expectations. In a private place, after a few minutes of touching, it is probably going to be a little too late to bring up the subject of putting the brakes on. "Stop" becomes just a word. By that point, **although "stop" means "stop,"** your hormones—those powerful, chemical messages from your body—will have taken over. It will be hard to even think straight.

So why not think now—when your hormones and your body aren't pressuring your mind—about what you want to do when you're alone with your crush? It will be less difficult to follow through with your convictions if you've thought about them ahead of time.

God is concerned about our whole being, and the Bible says don't be immoral. Your body is where God's Spirit lives. Sex is not only a body connection with someone; it's spiritual, too. The connection two people make during sex is designed to last forever.

Don't you know that your bodies are part of the body of Christ? Is it right for me to join part of the body of Christ to a prostitute? No, it isn't! Don't you know that a man who does that becomes part of her body? The Scriptures say, "The two of them will be like one person." But anyone who is joined to the Lord is one in spirit with him. Don't be immoral in matters of sex. That is a sin against your own body in a way that no other sin is. (1 Corinthians 6:15–18, CEV)

There's more to sex than mere skin on skin. Sex is as much spiritual mystery as physical fact. As written in Scripture, "The two become one." Since we want to become spiritually one with the Master, we must not pursue the kind of sex that avoids commitment and intimacy, leaving us more lonely than ever . . .

There is a sense in which sexual sins are different from all others. In sexual sin we violate the sacredness of our own bodies, these bodies that were made for God-given and God-modeled love, for "becoming one" with another. (1 Corinthians 6:16–18, MSG)

You hurt God's Spirit, which is living in you, when you have sex or enter into a "union" with someone you haven't committed to—someone you haven't taken vows to love and cherish forever. And you don't want to be connected forever to someone you may not even like tomorrow or next month! What you may feel for a special someone in a private moment or about a relationship right now isn't a good reason to make a sexual connection. You've heard it before, but the truth is God wants you to connect sexually once you're in a relationship that will last, which we consider marriage.

Reasons to Keep It in the Friend Zone

Write down reasons to wait to have sex.

_____

_____

_____

My Friend Zone Graph

It's a good idea to think about how far you want to go physically when approaching the boundaries of the Friend Zone with someone. This week, think about whether the following acts are okay when dating: holding hands, kissing, touching, lying down together, and _____.

(Add your own action words.)

Use this graph to chart the activities you feel are okay and not okay to do before marriage. Or create your own graph and, from left to right, write the activities, from the most to the least okay.

Hand Holding	Lip Kissing	French Kissing	Sex

Then, draw a horizontal line from the left to where your convictions say you will stop. When you are dating someone, review this chart together.

Write your thoughts on this below.

_____

_____

_____

_____

_____

BEATING TEMPTATION

You are tempted in the same way that everyone else is tempted. But God can be trusted not to let you be tempted too much, and he will show you how to escape from your temptations.
(1 Corinthians 10:13, CEV)

God knows that temptation exists and that you'll be faced with it. God will give you the strength to overcome temptation from your own strong feelings and the feelings of a partner you probably want to please. Dating presents heavy temptation. With God's help and by being intentional in dating, you can set yourself up to face less temptation and to be strong when you do encounter it.

It will help you enjoy the Friend Zone and ward off the temptation—and pitfall—of going beyond if you remember that God has a beautiful plan for your life. Acting in a way that pleases God now (Galatians 1:10) and honoring your Christian values will lead to that beautiful plan the Creator has for your life.

Do not be unequally bound together with unbelievers [do not make mismatched alliances with them, inconsistent with your faith]. For what partnership can righteousness have with lawlessness? Or what fellowship can light have with darkness? (2 Corinthians 6:14, AMP)

Set high standards for yourself. Know your boundaries. Know what qualities are important to you in a man. Remember a *boy*friend is not yet a man. Then, instead of being driven by impulses and feelings, you'll be prepared to make smart decisions. Enjoy this time in the Friend Zone, knowing you'll have plenty of time later for relationships. Many studies show that women are getting married later in life than they once did. You have tons of great experiences to enjoy now before you get involved in a romantic relationship that could preclude you from all the great adventures ahead. Wait and let romance and sex happen later, in God's time.

Know what you want in the future and be intentional about the company you keep now. Making sure not to bind yourself to someone who doesn't share your values keeps you open to a future partnership that can thrive.

Intentions

Meanwhile, here are some exercises to help you be prepared to enjoy this teen season of your life and overcome temptations that can pull you, before you're ready, into the next season.

Consider the statements below according to how important they are to you: "Not Important," "Somewhat Important," or "Deal Breaker." Circle your answer.

Name of person

_____

is a believer.	**Not Important / Somewhat Important / Deal Breaker**
goes to church with me.	**Not Important / Somewhat Important / Deal Breaker**
and I have similar relationship boundaries.	**Not Important / Somewhat Important / Deal Breaker**
is respectful of me always.	**Not Important / Somewhat Important / Deal Breaker**
is a hard worker.	**Not Important / Somewhat Important / Deal Breaker**
honors my feelings about sex and doesn't push or tease me.	**Not Important / Somewhat Important / Deal Breaker**
is kind to others.	**Not Important / Somewhat Important / Deal Breaker**

If you intend your future to be full, and someone is pressuring you to go beyond the boundaries you have set, it's time to break up! You are worthy of respect, and they need to abide by your boundaries without expecting you to *enforce* them. Only *yes* means yes, and no means no. And a person who respects you won't put you in a situation where you have to say no.

I Don't Know It All

Consider the statements below according to how important they are for *you*: "Not Important," "Somewhat Important," or "Deal Breaker." Circle your answer.

I honor the curfew my parents set.	**Not Important / Somewhat Important / Deal Breaker**
I'm honest with my parents about where I go and who I'm with.	**Not Important / Somewhat Important / Deal Breaker**
I discuss my plans with my parents.	**Not Important / Somewhat Important / Deal Breaker**
I don't let boys put their hands on me, because my body is sacred and touching leads to more.	**Not Important / Somewhat Important / Deal Breaker**
I am saving sex for marriage.	**Not Important / Somewhat Important / Deal Breaker**
I've had sex and decided I'm saving future sex for marriage.	**Not Important / Somewhat Important / Deal Breaker**

... love covers over a multitude of sins. (1 Peter 4:8, NIV)

Our Creator is a loving, forgiving God who can lift away the burden of our mistakes in everything, including dating.

A Boyfriend—To Choose or NOT?

The friend qualities in the previous chapter also apply to boys. Along with agreeing to the boundaries you've set, maybe this godly guy fits the future plans God has for you. What you do next is up to you, but be sure to consult God. They might be the *who* and even the *what*, but your teen years are probably not the *where* and *when* of God's relationship plan for you. Keep these thoughts in mind as you meditate on your ideal boyfriend qualities before choosing to pursue any relationship. In your relationship with your Lord, you'll have inner peace that can't be surpassed by any boyfriend relationship.

Be anxious for nothing, but in everything by prayer and supplication, with thanksgiving, let your requests be made known to God; and the peace of God, which surpasses all understanding, will guard your hearts and minds through Christ Jesus.
(Philippians 4:6–7, NKJV)

In the following columns, highlight the statements that would apply in your ideal relationship, whether you currently are dating someone or you're currently attached to your Divine Prince—Jesus. Jesus, by the way, is also called the Prince of Peace.

And His name will be called Wonderful, Counselor, Mighty God, Everlasting Father, Prince of Peace.
(Isaiah 9:6, NKJV)

COLUMN #1	COLUMN #2
When I'm having a bad day, he says, "Oh well. Get over it."	When I'm having a bad day, he says, "I am here for you if you need me." Then he sends me an inspirational text.
He never texts me until I text him.	He's always texting me and communicating in other ways.
He tells me that I'm ugly.	He tells me that I'm beautiful.
He constantly wants to push up on me, even when I ask him to stop.	He is a gentleman, and he refuses to even hold my hand without my permission.
He tells me to do things that defy my parents.	He is very respectful to my parents.
He tells me that he could get plenty of other girls.	He tells me he is lucky to be my friend.

COLUMN #1	COLUMN #2
He's tried to kiss me after I've said "no."	He's asked, "Can I kiss you?"
He's asked, "Don't you love me?"	He's said, "I love you."
He's said, "Send me a picture of your body."	He tells me that I'm a beautiful person.
He's asked, "Can we have sex?"	He's said he's keeping himself sexually pure.
He's asked, "Can you please keep it a secret?"	He's said, "No secrets."
He's said, "We can use protection."	He's said he's keeping himself sexually pure.
He's asked, "Can you just let me come over when your parents are not home?"	He's said, "Let's spend time together in public places."
He's asked, "Don't you want to have my baby?"	He's said, "I want to be a family man with a wife and children in the future. I don't want to risk that in any way."

If you highlighted *any* statements from Column #1, now is a good time to end the relationship. Make space for the godly friend God has planned for you!

Does He Treasure God?

For where your treasure is, there your heart will be also. (Matthew 6:21, NIV)

We give the majority of our concern and effort to what we value most. It's important that your friend loves the Lord as you do. This exercise will help you analyze if he treasures God (it will be a good self-exam for you, too). Answer by circling "True" or "False."

Name of person

_____

invites you to visit his church.	**True / False**
asked you if you believe in God or "are saved."	**True / False**
speaks positively about Jesus and references God in your conversations.	**True / False**
is focused on God, school, and being a good person.	**True / False**
likes to volunteer and serve.	**True / False**
is more concerned with your spiritual walk and less with your body.	**True / False**

If you circled "True" for three or more of the statements, you probably share faith in the Lord. This is a friendship that can grow as you invite each other to your churches and introduce each other to your youth pastors. If you circled "False" for three or more of the statements, consider how much you choose to invest in the relationship.

How Do I Know If My Parents Like My Boyfriend?

Children, you belong to the Lord, and you do the right thing when you obey your parents. The first commandment with a promise says, "Obey your father and your mother, and you will have a long and happy life." (Ephesians 6:1–3, CEV)

God tells us to honor our parents, and, as a result, we will have long and happy lives.

Part of honoring your parents, or whoever looks after you, is choosing to respect their input about dating. As independent as you might be feeling, God has promised his blessings on those who follow this instruction.

These are questions that will help you to determine whether your parents like your choice of friends (although it's probably not hard to tell). Write your answers on the line below each statement.

Did your parents ask to meet his parents?

_____

Have your parents allowed you to go out with him unaccompanied?

_____

Have your parents allowed you to go out with him in a group?

_____

Do your parents allow him to visit your house when they are home?

_____

Are you able to visit him at his house when his parents are home?

_____

Have your parents invited him to come over for dinner, or have they expressed openness to this?

_____

Once you've responded to these questions, sit down with your parents and discuss your answers. Be honest and respectful of their views. Show them your maturity and help them be more receptive to your friend.

If you remain in me and my words remain in you,
ask whatever you wish, and it will be done for you.
(John 15:7, NIV)

Is My Body My Temple?

All of you surely know that you are God's temple
and that his Spirit lives in you. Together you are
God's holy temple, and God will destroy anyone who
destroys his temple. (1 Corinthians 3:16–17, CEV)

You are a special creation, and your body is a temple of God. Therefore, it's a good decision to honor God with your body and choices in how you treat it. Your body is valued greatly by God, who will not take kindly to any wrongdoing against your body.

Ponder the following statements or questions, and then journal your responses.

These are situations where my body was not honored.

I felt pressured or uncomfortable when . . .

I felt good at the time, but I felt bad after . . .

Am I doing this for myself or someone else?

_____

If I go to this party, will I be pressured into behavior that might put my body at risk?

_____

Is this something Jesus would do or want me to do?

_____

What could result from our actions?

_____

Let this exercise serve as brainstorming for your social game plan to safeguard your body from harm. Write your plans in a journal, pray about them, and talk with a trusted friend or loved one who can help you keep your plans.

_____

_____

_____

_____

Mistakes and God's Forgiveness

Try this fill-in-the-blank exercise based on Scripture to see how sure you are in your knowledge of God's love and forgiveness for you. Choose from the words below to complete the sentences.

God forgives _____ *sins. (1 John 1:7)*

God will _____ *us or forsake us. (Deuteronomy 31:6)*

_____ *covers a multitude of sins. (1 Peter 4:8)*

God will never _____ *his back on me. (Hebrews 13:5)*

God said His _____ *is sufficient for me. (2 Corinthians 12:9)*

all	**loves**	**turn**	**mercy**
never leave	**love**	**grace**	

The Scripture references are given if you'd like to read more. Be comforted that even when things don't go according to plan or you make a bad decision, God's love for you never fails.

Pray, and God will continue to guide you to make dating decisions that honor your identity and worth. God answers those who pursue closeness with Him.

TO SUM UP

Be different. Put God first rather than trying to please any guy. God can offer you the strength you need to overcome inevitable temptation and help you stay true to the path that's right for you. Remember that God loves you, even if you've stumbled. Proverbs 24:16 says that although the righteous fall seven times, they rise again. God will continue to help you make better choices. You are God's child. God's love is unconditional and always remains. People place conditions on their love, but not God. Choose well whom you allow to get closest to you. The Lord will always take care of you. Stay focused on who God has called you to be, and know that your body is God's most precious cargo—always handle it with care.

Chapter 7

Preaching @ Me or Preaching to Me

But Jesus immediately said to them: "Take courage! It is I. Don't be afraid." (Matthew 14:27, NIV)

Who Is This?
Who heals all and never lets me fall.

Who Is This?
Who adds dividends to my dead ends.

Who Is This?
Who makes a way out of no way.

Who Is This?
Who loves me despite my sinful ways.

Who Is This?
Who holds me when I am hurt, never tells me a lie, and always unfolds the truth.

Who Is This?
Who lives within me and tells me that I will succeed with God.

His name is JESUS!

IS CHURCH FOR ME?

Instruct the wise and they will be wiser still; teach the righteous and they will add to their learning.
(Proverbs 9:9, NIV)

In other words, if you are knowledgeable, further teaching will make you more knowledgeable. If you live right and true to God's way, you'll learn even more.

Maybe you've been going to church your whole life with your family, and you love it. That's great! Or maybe you've been going with your family your whole life, and now you're getting to a point when you don't know if it's right for you. You love God and others, but does that really mean you have to go to church every week? You're busy with school and extracurriculars, and sleeping in one day a week is *sooo* good!

What if your parents never took you to church, but you wanted to go? Perhaps you love going to church, but you're no longer sure that your family's church is for you anymore. You're feeling stagnant there, or as if you're being preached at. Why so much preaching, anyway?

Whatever the case, this chapter will help refresh your mind and spirit about why church is important, so that you can make decisions about church that fuel your spiritual life and keep you on God's path for you. Even if you're comfortable in your faith, the Bible still instructs us to receive more guidance (Proverbs 9:9). As a young adult, it's not uncommon to feel the need to reevaluate your church life and recommit to churchgoing as your consciously chosen path—a decision you've made for yourself, not one that's been made for you. These types of decisions are an exciting part of coming into adulthood and taking ownership of your identity and faith.

Is church for you?

Just as a body, though one, has many parts, but all its many parts form one body, so it is with Christ. For we were all baptized by one Spirit so as to form one body—whether Jews or Gentiles, slave or free—and we were all given the one Spirit to drink. Even so the body is not made up of one part but of many.

Now if the foot should say, "Because I am not a hand, I do not belong to the body," it would not for that reason stop being part of the body. And if the ear should say, "Because I am not an eye, I do not belong to the body," it would not for that reason stop being part of the body. If the whole body were an eye, where would the sense of hearing be? If the whole body were an ear, where would the sense of smell be? But in fact God has placed the parts in the body, every one of them, just as he wanted them to be. If they were all one part, where would the body be? As it is, there are many parts, but one body.

The eye cannot say to the hand, "I don't need you!" And the head cannot say to the feet, "I don't need you!" On the contrary, those parts of the body that seem to be weaker are indispensable, and the parts that we think are less honorable we treat with special honor. And the parts that are unpresentable are treated with special modesty, while our presentable parts need no special treatment. But God has put the body together, giving greater honor to the parts that lacked it, so that there should be no division in the body, but that its parts should have equal concern for each other. If one part suffers, every part suffers with it; if one part is honored, every part rejoices with it.

Now you are the body of Christ, and each one of you is a part of it. (1 Corinthians 12:12-27, NIV)

This emphasizes the significance of people when it comes to church.

Is Church a Building?

To get a better sense of your feelings about church, highlight or circle any statements from the chart below that apply to you.

COLUMN #1	COLUMN #2
Can a building uplift me?	Can the church leader guide me throughout life?
Can a building preach the gospel to me?	Can my pastor help me understand the Bible?
Does a building help lead me to salvation?	Will I be able to witness to others about what I learned at church?
Can a building comfort me in my time of need?	Can I learn from different teachings at church?
Can a building shelter me emotionally?	Have the people at church supported and comforted me?
Can a building protect me from bullying?	Can my church family protect me from bullying if I ask for their help?
Does the building guide me through life?	Does church offer small groups to help me through life?

Have you highlighted everything from Column #2? Even if you highlighted most of Column #2, you understand the church exists inside of you. The people make up the church.

Open a conversation about this with a trusted adult mentor. Perhaps discuss ways you can choose to take a more active role in your church; after all, you are the future, and you have the power to help shape your church.

I Love It When . . .

It's time to get positive! This exercise will encourage you to think about what you love about being at church.

I love it when we _____ *at church.*

I love the people at church who act _____ *toward me.*

I love it when my parents _____ *at church.*

I love it when _____ .

I love it when _____ .

I love it when _____ .

How do you feel after this exercise? Did you find that there is more to love about your church than you realized? Share this exercise with a friend or loved one if you sense they're not feeling as excited about church as they could be. Discuss your struggles and renewed perspective together.

Are You Involved at Your Church?

> So then, as we have opportunity, let us do good to everyone, and especially to those who are of the household of faith. (Galatians 6:10, ESV)

It's the privilege and responsibility of believers to take part in God's work when we have the chance, especially in service to fellow believers. Choosing to share your unique capabilities at church will be a blessing to you and others.

Challenge: Ask your youth pastor at church how you can become more involved. Then, sign up to serve in a capacity that fits your gifts. Make a 21-day commitment to be the best leader, assistant, praise team member, etc. After each time you work in your position, be sure to journal about it. Remember to include your likes and dislikes about serving in that capacity. Did you like the position you took? How might this experience shape your decision to serve in the future?

Who Is the Creator to Me?

God is light; in him there is no darkness at all.
(1 John 1:5, NIV)

The Bible says a lot about the nature of God. God is called "light," fully devoid of darkness. God is all that is good and perfect and beautiful in existence. As a refresher in perspective about why church is important to your relationship with God, take a moment to consider who God is to you and why the relationship matters to you. We've covered a lot of Scripture about who God is. Let this exercise be about your personal experience with God. Answer on the lines provided.

God is my _____.

God makes me feel _____.

God expects _____ of me.

God has guided me through _____.

My relationship with God has meant _____ to me.

God has helped me make a tough decision, like _____.

When I spend time with God in prayer, I feel _____.

After a really powerful sermon at church, I feel _____.

If I don't pray for a while, I feel _____.

God has impacted my life in _____ *way.*

I've seen God shine through these people _____ *, and I want to be like them.*

If I didn't have God, it would mean _____ *for my life and future.*

I feel _____ *when I haven't been to church for a while.*

To get closer to God, I will choose to _____ *.*

Hopefully, this exercise brought to mind some positive feelings about your experience with God. Did you recall any fellow believers who have made a difference in your life? You can decide what to do with your feelings, but perhaps they will reignite your love of worship among your church community. You are all the church!

How to Find a Good Church Home

> My dear friends . . . I beg you to get along with each other. Don't take sides. Always try to agree in what you think. (1 Corinthians 1:10, CEV)

The Bible teaches unity in the minds and efforts of people for the Lord. Church should be a place of unity and where you feel you are among others who are driven for the same purposes. You should feel you belong there. Even if you are comfortable in your current church, perhaps you're curious about others' methods of worship and want to experience more. As long as your parents are okay with the decision, visiting other churches might be the right choice for you—and just the thing you need to get yourself excited about church.

Before you venture out, pray about it and do some research. Answer the questions that follow.

Are you interested in other denominations? Which ones, and what do you know about them?

What are the main characteristics in a church that you're looking to find? Are they contemporary music and a large youth group? Decide what you're most interested in seeing in your church.

_____

Can you commit to trying a church for more than one Sunday? This way, you'll give it a fair shot. It's hard to assess all aspects of what's going on at a church in one visit—even churches have "off" days!

_____

Here are some helpful questions you can ask a youth pastor while you are visiting different churches:

1. Do you have student-driven activities?

_____

2. Do you have summer camps for all ages?

_____

3. Do you recommend any classes that will give me a better understanding of the Bible?

_____

4. How many students are in your youth group? How many students do you have in my grade level? (This is an important question because you can gauge whether you prefer a smaller or larger setting.)

_____

5. Do you encourage student involvement?

_____

TO SUM UP

Proverbs 11:25 (NIV) says, "A generous person will prosper; whoever refreshes others will be refreshed." And Psalm 32:8 (NIV) says, "I will instruct you and teach you in the way you should go; I will counsel you with my loving eye on you." Likewise, a good pastor or youth leader will be generous in spirit, lift others up, and aim to look after their congregation or pupils. The benefit of godly instruction and care in a pastor is priceless for your life and ability to make godly decisions. I pray that you have or will soon find that guidance. Keep letting that desire be known to God. The Almighty will lead you there or help you see your current church for its good and be renewed in the love and spirit filling its walls.

As mentioned before, God is not one who will force a belief or decision upon you. So, when others try to push a decision about anything on you, even church or religion, don't feel forced. By now, you're probably sensing that the Creator wants you to come on your own. Jesus is not going to be pushy, nor will Jesus be forceful, he's just waiting for you with open arms. Life is your personal spiritual journey.

God's love happens organically. God doesn't show up and then disappear. The Almighty will come into every corner of your life when you invite the Holy Spirit in. With Jesus, you will feel confident, strong, and at peace while you make decisions that lead to total spiritual health. Remember to speak up if someone is forceful about God or church. God's word is powerful on its own. God is light and love. A good teacher will present God's word to you lovingly.

Chapter 8

My Future Looks Brighter

I will bless you with a future filled with hope—a future of success, not of suffering. (Jeremiah 29:11, CEV)

A Beautiful Walk

A spiritual walk is what I'm on.
I'm standing firm and standing strong.
God is with me through and through.
The Lord is my everything; I thought you knew.

If you call on God, you will see,
he walks with you
as he walks with me.

Times are hard but my walk is strong.
A spiritual walk is what I'm on.
I do not care what others think
when my God agrees—that's enough for me.

So get on this path if you want to be free.
The spiritual path is good. You'll see.
Just take a spiritual walk.

BELIEVE

Although, at times, life may have you sad and thinking the worst or have you grappling with tough decisions, God has a wonderful plan for your future. We can be sure that the best is yet to come for us because of the promise of God's word.

Do You Believe in Yourself?

Complete the sentences with the words below.

I believe that I was _____ in_____

image. The plans God has for me are _____. My future is

_____ with _____ as my Lord

and _____. Without the _____

I am nothing, but with the _____, I am everything. I believe

that my life is better when I follow guidelines set by Jehovah.

created	**brighter**	**creator**	**Jesus**
God's	**Jehovah**	**savior**	**limitless**

Hopefully, this paragraph will have you believing that you can do anything.

Are My Plans in Life Better Than the Plans God Has for Me?

The Lord wants your devotion. God has a plan for you and promises you great blessings in exchange for your commitment and for whatever you feel you sacrifice in the process (Mark 10:29–30). Consider whether you still believe your plans are better than God's plans. If you believe yours are better, explain how. If not, explain your reason.

My plans in life are better plans than God has for me because

_____

My plans in life are not better plans than God has for me because

_____

_____

If you're conflicted about whose plans you think are best for your life, pray about it and seek the guidance of a trusted adult. You will make the right decision about whose plans to follow for your best future.

Promises and Trust

It's a big deal to choose to devote your entire life to God. It requires a lot of trust.

This exercise is about building up your trust in God with Scripture. Read the following Scriptures aloud:

The Lord will fight for me; I need only to be still. (Exodus 14:14)

The Lord will strengthen me and help me. (Isaiah 41:10)

The Lord says that when I pass through the waters, He will be with me; and when I pass through the rivers, they will not sweep over me. When I walk through the fire, I will not be burned; the flames will not set me ablaze. (Isaiah 43:2)

The Lord our God wants me to humble myself and pray. (2 Chronicles 7:14)

How do you feel when you read of God's promises to help, protect, and be with you? It sounds amazing, yes? Do you trust what you read? If you're struggling, talk to God about it in prayer. Don't miss out on what is truly available to you through trust in God.

_____

_____

_____

_____

Making Godly Decisions for What's Next

As you move through your teen years, make them count with good and godly decisions that will ensure a wonderful future. You have already come so far, and the best is yet to come.

Here are some decisions to consider that will help you take another step toward future-casting. Think them over, then write your ideas on the lines provided.

1. **Decide Your Priorities (Weekly and Monthly).** You have already gotten into the practice of thinking about your daily priorities, but now it's time to start looking at longer-term priorities. Jot down a few important things you can do this and every week and this and every month through high school. At the start of the week and month, journal about it or write your priorities in a planner. This exercise will have you making active decisions that will move you closer to where you want to be in the future.

_____

_____

_____

_____

2. **What's Not a Priority?** Sure, teen life is full of academic and family pressure, and you're busy working on developing your faith life—not to mention you need friends and fun! Think about what's not a priority right now and whether there are activities you could cut or scale back on.

_____

_____

_____

_____

3. **Take Time to Relax and Pray.** With the ideas in this book, hopefully you've discovered some self-care practices that work for you. Write down a plan for establishing your favorite rest and recharge activities as regular occurrences. How does time with God fit into this scenario?

_____

_____

_____

_____

4. **Talk to People Who Have Been There.** As you start to think more about your future and goals, talk to older people about their paths. What choices had the best impact on their lives—choosing a church, deciding a major in college, taking a particular job, or volunteering? Learn what you can from others who have faced the decisions you're facing.

_____

_____

_____

_____

5. **Write Down Your Own Plan.** God will help you get where you're supposed to be. List some steps you're choosing to take to reach your spiritual, physical, educational, and professional goals for the future. Pray for continued guidance and trust in God's support.

_____

_____

_____

_____

TO SUM UP

God wants to give you a future that's brighter than can be imagined. If you put your trust in God, you are capable of so much more in your life than is possible by yourself or with the help of other humans.

You don't have to bear your burdens alone. Try not to lean just on your own understanding (Proverbs 3:5). Decisions at this time in life are tough, and so much is riding on them, but God will direct your path. A successful future is achieved through faith—a person with the faith of a tiny seed can achieve big goals (Matthew 17:20).

I pray that the exercises and inspiration in this book have already begun to help you maneuver through life's hard decisions, keeping God as your director and leader. I urge you to always put God first. God's best is the best for you. You are destined for greatness. Make great decisions and go forth in greatness.

Spiritual growth is expressed in more ways than in words. Use this page to express yourself by coloring, drawing, doodling or other graphics.

BIBLICAL CITATIONS

ABOUT THE AUTHOR

Jocasta "Ma Ma J" Odom is a woman with many hats, but her largest and most rewarding hat is being the mother of two handsome boys. She has a BS in biology and an MBA with a specialization in health care management, and she teaches middle school science. Jocasta is also the author of *Transformation* and is the owner and designer of the custom bow tie collection Quo-Ties.

In 2002, Jocasta founded the women's organization Beloved Sistah Circle. She is a certified spiritual life coach who is focused on her clients' transformation. She is an ordained minister. Jocasta is an excellent motivational speaker whose truth takes her audience to another level. She was a radio personality for four years on 108 Praise Radio and had her own show called *That's What's Up*. She also had an inspirational segment on WATC sharing Scripture and God-given motivation and is currently a host on WATC's *Atlanta Live*.

Jocasta is a former reality star from the CBS hit show *Big Brother*. She is also an actress and toured with Vanessa Nartey's *Unshame On You*; performed in two of Chadwick Lloyd's plays: *Heaven, Heartache, and the Power of Love* and *Heaven, Heartache, and the Power of Christmas*; and has done commercials.

Jocasta loves to give back. She strives to reach people through motivation, poetry, preaching, and teaching what God wants told. Jocasta has learned through several trials how her life should be, so she has vowed to show others what she has learned.

Jocasta Odom
jocastabookings@gmail.com
www.jocastaodom.com

9 781646 111275